STEALING THE MARKET

OTHER BOOKS ON FINANCIAL SUBJECTS
BY MARTIN MAYER

STEALING
THE
MARKET

How the Giant
Brokerage Firms, with Help from the
SEC, Stole the Stock Market
from Investors

MARTIN MAYER

BasicBooks
A Division of HarperCollinsPublishers

Library of Congress Cataloging–in–Publication Data
Mayer, Martin, 1928–
    Stealing the market: how the giant brokerage firms, with help from the SEC, stole the stock market from investors/ Martin Mayer.
        p. cm.
    Includes bibliographical references and index.
    ISBN 0–465–05362–9
    1.   Stockbrokers—United   States—Corrupt   practices.
2. Securities industry—United States—Corrupt practices.
3.   Stock-exchange–United   States—Corrupt   practices.
4. Securities fraud—United States. I. Title.
HG4928.5.M39 1992
364.1'68—dc20   91–55600
                                                            CIP

Copyright © 1992 by Martin Mayer
PRINTED IN THE UNITED STATES OF AMERICA
Designed by Ellen Levine
92 93 94 95 96 SWD/RRD 9 8 7 6 5 4 3 2 1

For William W. Prager, my mother's brother,
a contributor to the 1936 SEC
*Report on the Feasibility and Desirability
of the Complete Segregation of the Functions of Broker and Dealer,*
and one of the last great gentlemen,
for his ninetieth birthday.

Contents

Acknowledgments

This book began as a Twentieth Century Fund study, commissioned by the late Murray Rossant, who died before it could be completed. A former economics correspondent for *The New York Times* and one of the anonymous authorities of *The Economist*, Murray knew and cared about the markets. The investment guru Leo Model was among his closest friends. I once accused him of wanting to be president of a foundation because he loved the idea of managing the investment portfolio, and he didn't entirely deny it.

Murray's temporary successor knew nothing of markets and cared less, and my project was in many ways a problem for her. Part of the problem was that foundation money goes to "writers" rather than "professors" because the foundations want something the public will find approachable, and "writers" take what are usually unprofitable commissions from foundations because they want the chance to write for a more knowledgeable audience. Another part was that Murray, who was a friend, had commissioned from me something rather different from the project he had presented to his distinguished board of directors, and there was little documentation in the files. The board, and

Murray's successor, had envisioned a pamphlet about "insider trading," Ivan Boesky, Dennis Levine, and the like, a subject Murray and I thought inherently uninteresting for all its flashy topicality. What mattered systemically in the late 1980s, we agreed, was *market* inside information, knowledge of what the institutions were doing, which their brokers were using against them.

The decision to move this project from foundation sponsorship to commercial publication was greatly facilitated by Martin Kessler's decision—after reading the admittedly rather quirky manuscript I had written for the Fund—that there really was a book here and that Basic Books would wish to publish it. I agreed, at first reluctantly but finally with complete conviction, that the book had to be started again from scratch, and no more than twenty or thirty pages of the Twentieth Century Fund manuscript have in fact survived to publication here. The approach and much of the information are the same, however, and the conclusions are still to some degree informed by my conversations with Murray in the mid- and late 1980s.

The subject was exotic in 1988, and among those who wanted no part of it were the Securities and Exchange Commission (SEC) (which was quite willing to see the brokers violate fiduciary obligations if only they would contribute to the liquidity of the market) and the New York Stock Exchange (which knew that damage was being done but could not act against its own mighty barons). By 1991, the rot in the markets was more visible, and the NYSE was beginning to understand the disaster that lies ahead. Thus it is possible to thank NYSE chairman William Donaldson, vice-chairman Donald Stone, president Richard Grasso, and chief economist James Cochrane for their help in the final stages of the work. (In fairness, it is probably more my fault than his that I did not spend more than a few minutes with Donaldson's predecessor John Phelan.) I am indebted to Gedale Horowitz of Salomon Brothers, chairman of the Securities Industries Association in 1991. Also to Mary McCue of the SEC, who shares with Peter Bakstansky of the Federal Reserve Bank of New York the black belt as world's champion press representative for a government agency. Both are far too professional to let their work be influenced by what they or their bosses may think of the approach a reporter is taking to a story.

While the subject was still unpopular, I had significant help from John J. Morton, Richard Heckman, John Mendelson, Laszlo Birinyi, Jr., David Silver, Roberta Karmel, Stephen A. Berkowitz, Stanley Abel, Eugene Noser, Gordon Macklin and Gene Finn of the National Association of Securities Dealers (NASD), Pearce Bunting and his staff at the Toronto Stock Exchange, Stanley Beck of the Ontario Securities Commission, Wayne Wagner of Plexus, Andre Villeneuve of Reuters USA, George McNamee of First Albany, Harry Keefe, and colleagues on the Office of Technology Assessment Panel on Securities Markets and Information Technology—especially Eric Clemons, Peter Schwartz, David Hale, Manning Warren III, William Brodsky, and John Bachman of Edward D. Jones. SEC Chairman Richard Breeden and Commissioner Joseph Grundfest were generous with their time. Scott Pardee, Peter Carney, Michael Bloomberg, John Schmidt, John Oros, and Steven Wunsch were significantly helpful at the end. Jean-François Bernheim and I argue out some of these subjects at regular intervals, and I learn from the arguments. Charles Ramond keeps me up to date on foreign exchange markets. There are a number of people who work on the floor of the New York Stock Exchange who were helpful both in general and in particular, but who would not care to be named.

This is my fifth book dealing with aspects of the securities business in the United States. The earliest of them was written in 1952 and 1953. My indebtedness thus goes back to others who contributed to my education in these matters over a period that now exceeds forty years. It is almost impossible (I wish I could say it is entirely impossible) to write about these subjects without making errors, especially if the effort is to understand how things happen and why people do what they do, and these failures of my education must be blamed on the student rather than on his teachers.

CHAPTER 1

Why the Stock Market Matters

When the former Gold Coast became Ghana in 1957, the first of the British colonies to take independence, its leader Kwame Nkrumah staged a monster party in the capital city of Accra. The central event of the night after the formal transfer of power was a theatrical presentation in the athletic stadium by the graduating class of the best boys' high school in the country. They put on Aristophanes' *The Frogs*, in Greek. Among those in attendance as part of the U.S. delegation was Ralph Flynt, an associate commissioner of education, a balding, lean, tall drink of water from Virginia, who walked out, partly because he had no Greek and was bored, partly because he was disgusted that a country which desperately needed engineers and technicians put the flower of its educational enterprise into classical languages.

From the viewpoint of the fighters for Ghanaian independence, however, the performance made plentiful sense. They had spent years wondering what fault in their stars had made them underlings, and they had found a perfectly plausible answer. What did the Englishman have that the African did not have? He had Greek. Greek was the white man's juju. The black man would learn Greek, and would inherit the earth. These children were the vanguard, and thus the most fitting to hail the new era.

For the reformers of the Soviet Union and the leaders of the newly liberated countries of Eastern Europe, the New York Stock Exchange is the Americans' juju. They do not really know what the orators are saying in the old agora, it's all Greek to them, but they recognize the capitalist god. A stock exchange represents the capitalist pantheon: market pricing, investment, speculation, *making money.*

In fairness, the stock market has juju qualities in the United States, too. Because the exchanges are so open and because the prices of what they trade are incessantly fluctuating (as J. P. Morgan advised when asked by a reporter what he thought the market would do in the next few months: "It will fluctuate," he said), the exchanges are the natural newsmakers of the economy from the point of view of the news purveyors. The Monday evening news on the networks tells people how much the Dow Jones Industrial Averages went up or down that day, but not, for example, the rates at that day's weekly auction of U.S. Treasury bills—though the money spent to buy the T-bills just at this one weekly auction exceeds the total trading in the Dow in the entire $32\frac{1}{2}$ hours that the market is open each week.

The mythology that surrounds the stock market makes it difficult for the public, the government, and even the academic community to deal intelligently with what is indeed one of the important *but not central* institutions of a capitalist economy. Investment and employment in the real economy are in truth affected, as we shall see, by the movement of prices on the stock exchange and the devices by which people with an interest in those prices seek to influence and profit by those movements. But these effects are indirect and long-term. In terms of what will happen tomorrow, or next month, or even in the next election, the Monday T-bill auctions not only involve more money than a week's transactions in the thirty Dow Industrial stocks, they also give more useful information about where we are as a political economy and where we are heading. (Perhaps one should note in passing, too, that the Dow Averages are really a nutty number: Stock splits have made the multiplier a minor fraction, which means that a move of $1 in the shares of each of the thirty companies on the Dow list will produce a move of more than 50 points in the averages. And the Dow measurement is an *average:* each of the thirty stocks carries the same weight, though their capitilizations are very different.)

Moreover, as 1987 proved (both in the run-up of the first nine months and the crash of the tenth), stock markets can accept, process, and pass on very poor information. Share prices can become disconnected from the real world. And some of this mispricing is systemic. Tax laws distort the relationship between the return to debt-holders and the return to shareholders, strongly influencing the price of both stocks and bonds. Other legal anomalies permit controlling shareholders to abuse corporate assets in ways that make the ownership of the whole company worth much more in proportion than the ownership of its pieces, leading to the strange phenomenon of the leveraged buy-out, which made so few so rich in the 1980s and so many so poor in the next decade.

Professors of finance have reinforced the natural tendency of corporations to borrow rather than to save or issue new stock (which would dilute the ownership of current shareholders), and have driven to unprecedented heights the ratio of debt to equity in the American economy. Dogma associated with the names of Franco Modigliani of the Massachusettes Institute of Technology and Merton Miller of the University of Chicago stated that for corporate planning purposes debt and equity were essentially equivalent, because bankruptcy was so uncommon that its consequences could be ignored. Michael Jensen of the Harvard Business School argued that failure to service debts acquired on a junk bond chassis would not impose bankruptcy on the issuers, anyway. Few leveraged buy-outs, he claimed, "ever enter formal bankruptcy. They are reorganized quickly . . . and at much lower costs."[1]

On the "buy side" of the market, other finance professors, by stressing the overriding value of diversification, have justified admittedly (indeed, proudly) brainless behavior by money managers, with significant effect on the movement of prices in the stock markets.

For those who follow the cliché to "investigate, then invest," and who weigh corporate earnings and assets before committing their money, leading accountants have provided misleading reports of corporate earnings and net worth by the development of arcane devices that take the bad news off the profit-and-loss statement. Somehow the profitable activities are always recurring, and naturally appear as part of earnings from ongoing operations; but the losing activities are one-shots, and can be taken onto the balance sheet via a footnote without passing through the p&l.

Except in Britain, where legal constraints on corporate governance often compel companies to raise money by giving their shareholders "rights" to buy new shares at prices below the current market, stock exchanges are not places where corporations find new capital. Even companies that are raising money by selling stock do it in underwritings away from the normal market mechanisms. (The companies sell their stock to an underwriter, and get their money whether or not the underwriter can sell to the public at the offering price.) It is to some extent, of course, a distinction without a difference, because without a stock market on which new shares can be resold by their original purchasers, the companies would find it all but impossible to get the underwriters interested. And, obviously, the prices of existing shares determine how much money corporations can raise by selling new shares.

Still, securities markets are far from essential for the financing of capitalist enterprise. Germany and Japan rose from the ashes of World War II with financing systems that made bank loans rather than sales of shares (or bonds) the source of investment capital. It is by no means clear that Brazilian economic growth would have been more balanced (it could not have been faster) if the source of funds had been a market for the investment of deliberate household and corporate savings rather than allocation by parastatal industrial enterprise of the "savings" forced on a society by inflation. The Ford Motor Company was wholly owned by the Ford family (and then its foundation) until the 1950s, and grew in its glory days mostly by pyramiding its own retained profits. IBM didn't issue new stock for thirty years, until Thomas J. Watson, Sr., the man who built it, died. The electronics industry on Boston's Route 128 was started by Laurance Rockefeller and his family, not by groups of anonymous investors who took a flier on technology stocks; Bing Crosby financed Minute Maid. National

City Bank of New York staked Aristotle Onassis (whose enterprises flourished without ever selling a share of stock), lending him the money—just about all the money—to buy his first tanker.

It can be cogently argued that stock exchanges exist not because they are needed, but because people *want* them. As the economist Hyman Minsky has long insisted, the really important investment decisions in the United States have always been made by the lending officers of commercial banks rather than by the "investment bankers" who sell shares and bonds to the public. Indeed, the disaster of the junk bond issuance in the 1980s was that it took away from the banks the kind of investment decision that had previously been made by bankers who expected long-term relationships with the borrowers. One can also argue, by the way, that this development led to the atrophy of credit judgment at the large banks, which created the banking crisis of the 1990s.

The brilliance of Drexel Burnham, and the malfunctioning of the markets which that brilliance invented and exploited, created a new context for borrowing by companies in the "middle market," companies with annual sales of $25 million to $100 million—and new opportunities for their proprietors and CEOs to achieve glory. Much borrowing that would have been done through banks was pushed into the hands of investment houses that earned fees and quick profits by peddling paper to institutions with little interest in the borrowers' business.[2] But these were atomized "transactions" that ended when the profit was booked. Later, when the loan went bad and the borrower needed a banker to restructure it, what he had instead was the indenture of a bond, containing terms that were legally a contract between the company and those who owned its paper. Such terms could not be changed without the consent of the bondholders.

Finally, stock markets are by their nature somewhat "inefficient"—that is, the prices of the securities traded in these markets may be susceptible to movements that do not reflect the success or failure of the companies that issued the shares and the industries of which they are a part. John Maynard Keynes commented years ago that stock prices are controlled not by the projected earnings of the companies but by market expectations of those earnings. Indeed, the most widely accepted academic school of financial analysis, not in the least Keynesian in its orientation, holds that nobody can, acting solely on the basis of publicly available information, predict which stocks will do better or which will do worse than the average stock traded in the market over the next months. The corollary to that, hugely damaging to the efficiency of our markets, is that nothing counts in the equation but the denominator, the short-term rate of interest dictated by the Federal Reserve System, which determines the discount rate a market oriented to the short term will apply to projected earnings.

By far the fastest growing form of investment in equity securities in the 1980s was the "index fund," which owned stocks in proportion to their weighting in the Standard & Poor's index of 500 stocks. If enough of those stocks went up in a day's trading, the index went up and the price of the fund went up. If enough of them went down, the index went down and the price of the fund went down. In the early 1980s, indexes themselves became tradable (as "derivative" instruments, futures, or option contracts with values that were functions of the movement of this measurement of the price movements among the underlying stocks).

We shall look later at the system of "index arbitrage" by which movements in the price of the index itself were communicated to the price of the stocks that made up the index. For now let us note that on January 9, 1991, a day when the Dow fell forty points, Blockbuster Entertainment was the second most heavily traded stock on the New York Stock Exchange, and its price rose by 9 percent, though overcapacity in the video rental business had made such companies a dubious investment. On that day, Pan Am had to be removed from the S&P index because it had filed for bankruptcy, and S&P chose Blockbuster as a suitable substitute. All the index funds then had to buy Blockbuster to keep their holdings identical to the index list, and the new demand naturally goosed the price of the stock, probably preventing the index from falling quite as far as it would have fallen otherwise.[3]

Why should anyone care that stock prices get pushed around by the malfunctioning of an exchange? Surely the American stock markets—the over-the-counter market that operates on telecommunications lines as well as the market that happens on a trading floor—are the best places in the world to conduct financial business: public, "transparent" (that is, the world can see what's going on), professionally supervised. From the point of view of large institutional investors that play the various bond, interest rate, and currency markets, the stock markets have a warm, secure, almost down-home feeling. The foreign exchange market, as travelers learn in a small way when they go abroad and have to change their currency, is rigged for the dealers in a large way. Most trading among the big currency dealers (primarily the multinational banks) is done through a Reuters computer that connects buyers and sellers and then disappears from the circuit, keeping no record of the trade. (Dealers do record their telephone conversations for their own protection, but the recordings are destroyed after the transactions are confirmed.) In 1990, Reuters launched a new and improved system that *would* keep records, making it at least conceivable that the banks' customer could find out what the bank paid for the currency and thus how large a markup the customer had been charged. Nobody used it; the whole point of being a dealer in the foreign exchange market was that the ultimate purchaser or seller whose order had triggered the transaction could never find an audit trail.

The government bond market, another place where no publicity is given to the price at which paper is actually bought and sold, is a notorious minefield for innocent municipal pension fund managers. Their custom is worth so much to the government bond dealers that the people who run these funds can come to town and get absolutely any entertainment they want, free of charge, from their friendly government bond dealers. The "interdealer broker" screens on which the forty-odd "primary dealers" make their bids and offers for government bonds are absolutely restricted to those primary dealers. It doesn't matter how large your holdings of government bonds are and how important a role you play in the market, you can't buy access to an interdealer broker screen. In 1989, RMJ Securities, one of those brokers, tried to offer the quotes on its screens to other than primary dealers and was promptly boycotted by all those whose quotes made the market.

And "for all its faults," as Edward Wyatt wrote in *Barron's*, "when compared to publicly available information in the corporate and municipal bond markets, the government bond arena looks like the Library of Congress."[4] Arthur Levitt, while

president of the American Stock Exchange in the 1970s, said of
the municipal bond market that it was "like an Oriental bazaar,"
and it still is. The self-enforcing processes of market regulation
that infuse the exchanges simply do not exist in these markets.
Why worry about the pimples just below the lacquered surface of
the open-and-above-board stock exchange, when these larger
blisters are hidden behind the opacity of the currency and
government markets?

To which there are two answers. The first is that the corruption
in the bond and foreign exchange markets is not very interesting.
Like the "insider trading" that got so much attention in the
1980s, it is a declarative sentence: Some People Are Cheating.
Moreover, while technology and the creation of derivative markets
have diminished the transparency and honesty of the stock market,
they have created the conditions for more reputable markets in
bonds and foreign exchange. The development of an artificial
Treasury bond for futures trading has already deprived dealers of
the opportunity to exploit and perhaps create price differences
between government bonds with essentially identical terms that
happen to mature in different years; the futures contracts on
currencies (the original commoditized financial contracts, dating
back to 1972) have taken from the banks the lucrative
opportunities to fiddle that were inherent in that market when the
banks' customized "forward" contracts were the only game in
town for the exporter/importer. In the very near future,
syndicated services will supply to the buyers and sellers of these
instruments much better information than they have today.
Indeed, Bloomberg Financial Information, the most rapidly
growing electronic publishing operation in America, has already
blown much of the fog out of the bond markets. In any case,
there is now so much money flowing through these channels
(literally hundreds of billions of dollars a day) that the insiders can
live very well on the proceeds of only the teeniest bit of fiddling.

Resolving the cheating in the bond and forex markets,
moreover, would not require significant systemic change. The
problems here could be eliminated under existing legislation, with
no major changes in the ways business is done, if the securities and
banking regulators wished to do the work (and, perhaps, if they
were smart enough). One can even have some sympathy with the

attitude of these regulators, that they don't want to and shouldn't have to do the work, that the "buy side" in the foreign exchange and government bond markets—the giant corporations and multinational banks and institutional investors—are big boys who can take care of themselves, or hire their own cops and sue for fraud if it turns out they've been taken. In the real world, things work otherwise, but the attitude is not an unreasonable one for bureaucrats and academics who tend to have a limited understanding of the hurly-burly of real commercial life.

The second reason to take the stock market as a more troublesome locus of ethical backsliding and systemic mispricing is the pervasive nature of the price information that emerges from that market. The symbolic importance of these prices in the minds of the informed as well as the naive grossly exceeds their real role in the economy. Rentiers, most of them rather small and not very rich rentiers, feel safe or sorry according to the values asserted for their holdings in the daily market reports. A rising market bespeaks prosperity, and an active stock market with heavy public participation shows faith in the honesty and fairness of economic institutions.

Over time, for all the errors, prices in an open, honest, and transparent stock market will give to the decision-makers of an economy guidance far better than the guidance available from the study of government statistics or the reports of academic researchers. Comparative price/earnings ratios especially provide essential clues as to which industries (and companies within industries) are on their way up or down. An industry where price/earnings multiples are high (where the public is willing to pay many times the current profits for the right to a share of future profits) will be able to raise new investment capital easily and cheaply; an industry where price/earnings multiples are low may be virtually frozen out of the capital markets, like the banks in 1990. In the case of the banks, of course, courtesy the accountants and the federal banking regulators, the earnings claimed were clearly an artifact of the tools used to measure them, and it may well be that the market in fall 1990 was awarding the banks a perfectly reasonable and even generous price/earnings ratio as related to the true earnings.

In the stock market as in politics, where a man stands is a

function of where he sits. For the market to be a guide to those who make real (as distinguished from merely financial) investment decisions, the buyers and sellers of stocks must be drawn from a community large enough to provide a varied collection of seats. The higher the fraction of the nation's stock ownership concentrated in a relatively few institutional holders, pension funds and mutual funds, insurance companies and bank trust departments, the more likely that price movements will relate to computer-generated statistics rather than individual analysis of the company and how it's doing. The computers are probably smarter than the people, but they all use the same programs and process the same information. People will disagree far more often than computers. And it's difference of opinion that makes markets, as well as horse races.

If in fact a small number of experts armed with computers and official information could make better decisions on the allocation of resources than markets make, command economies would outperform market economies. My master Wassily Leontief, when he began creating his input-output grid in the 1940s (for the U.S. Air Force, by the way), thought that his system would indeed permit planning procedures far superior to the vagaries of market-derived information. He was wrong, as he has since admitted, although he still thinks we plan too little. In the end, in complex societies, there is no substitute for market information.

Finally, the stock exchange, to a much greater extent than is generally recognized, represents the moral side of capitalism, for stock exchanges can operate successfully only in an atmosphere of trust and openness. Commodity exchanges are anonymous places, planned so that traders are protected from those with whom they trade by the exchange's clearinghouse. (After a transaction is completed in a commodity "pit," buyer and seller have separate contracts with the clearinghouse, rather than a contract with each other.) "Commodity exchanges are designed to permit trading among strangers," said Terence Martell, the research director for Comex, the New York exchange that trades silver and gold, "as distinguished from stock exchanges, which are designed to permit only trading among friends." A stock exchange is necessarily a kind of club.

In a stock market, a man's word really is his bond. In theory—

and the theory is theoretically backed by the rules of the establishment—only fiduciaries, people acting in the interests of their principals and not for their own profit, can execute public orders; without specific exemptions, they cannot trade for their own account while calling or accepting bids and offers for the same stock from members of the public. The ultimate purchaser operates on trust, that the broker has well and truly represented his interest in executing his order—and the broker dealing with that customer must follow rules that forbid him to recommend any investment not "suitable" for this customer. The broker operates on trust: If his customer does not pay for what he bought, or deliver what he sold, the broker nevertheless must make good on the deal out of his own funds. Finally, all trades must be reported, price and size and precisely when. On American stock exchanges, the bids and offers are public knowledge, available to anyone with the subscription price of a Quotron or one of the rival services. And until 1991, the reports of trades were to all intents and purposes instantaneous and universal: No buyer or seller could know about a completed transaction any faster than any other buyer or seller.

The thesis of this book is that we are in the process of losing all the advantages of the stock market system. More and more trading is done away from the exchanges, in back alleys whence no report emerges, by players who act in their own interest, gaining the information on which they act from clients who believe they are communicating with their agents. When a publicly held investment house trades for its own account while processing orders in the same stocks from its clients, it operates, as Norman Poser of the American Stock Exchange said some years ago, not under a conflict of interest but under a conflict of *duties*.

Some people think this is a dandy result. In *Barron's* for October 15, 1990, L. Gordon Crovitz of *The Wall Street Journal* acclaims a new SEC rule that permits large institutions to buy and sell certain kinds of securities from and to each other and their brokers without telling anybody about it. He likes the rule precisely *because* it will over time, as it gets extended, establish a "two-tier" securities market, where the prices paid by individuals on the exchange may have little or no relation to the prices institutions and the large investment houses pay each other.[5]

"Having determined that the complexity of the market and its products are [sic] beyond their attention or skill level," securities lawyer Saul Cohen wrote in early 1991, individuals "are voting to depart as direct investors and reinvest in mutual funds or pension plans." At the brokerage houses, he continues, "marketing now aims to have their representatives bring customer assets in house for professional management, rather than provide individual advice. . . . [W]ith the individual investor fleeing the market, regulation in his interest will be seen even by regulators to be a huge waste of the public money." Cohen admired the London Stock Exchange, which had done away first with its trading floor and then with its requirement that dealers report all trades: "Its opaqueness and efficiency is [sic] valuable to institutions."[6]

We shall have occasion in the succeeding chapters to take these contentions apart one at a time. The decision of the brokerage houses to sell their clientele products rather than services grows out of the shift from the partnership to the corporate form, and the demand from the firms' own stockholders for a greater degree of stability in earnings than the delivery of personal services can promise. People save through pension funds rather than with personally managed investments mostly because the earnings of a pension fund are tax-exempt, and pension funds are the most aggressive traders in the modern stock markets because their trading profits are also tax-exempt. The growth of London's opaque and supposedly efficient market has inevitably been accompanied by the collapse of an increasing number of the "unit trusts" (British for "mutual funds") that were supposed to provide the "professional management" Cohen finds an entirely satisfactory alternative to open and honest markets—and in these collapses, incidentally, investors typically lost *everything*. Looking back on the five years since the Big Bang that fused the broker and dealer functions in London, *The Financial Times* found fund managers "bewailing the passing of an era when one's word was one's bond."[7]

The most important objection to Cohen's position, however, is that no public purpose is served by a securities market that fails to publish the details of its transactions in a time frame short enough to permit those who were not participants in the transactions to gain by the information. These markets do not exist to make people rich, or to reduce the contributions employers are required to make to pension funds, or even to facilitate transactions; they exist to help decision-makers in the real, nonfinancial economy to determine where the nation's savings should be invested. What has been happening to our securities markets since the 1960s—in small increments, driven by changes in data processing and communications technology, business practice, sociology, and government—has come to the edge of tragedy.

As this book goes to press in fall 1991, the Securities and Exchange Commission has taken two steps that make tragedy more likely. Though trading in stocks by large institutions serves no economic purpose, relating more closely to movements in the price of index futures than to analyses of the prospects of individual companies, the SEC in September joined the Treasury Department in asking Congress for changes in the tax code that would remove all inducements to mutual funds to invest rather than to trade their shareholders' money. And in October the Commission pointed a dagger at the heart of the Securities Acts its members are sworn to enforce, permitting the National Association of Securities Dealers to exempt its members from public reporting of their purchases and sales in early morning trading sessions the SEC authorized to begin in January 1992. Floyd Norris of *The New York Times* called the decision an "assault on the public's right to know. . . . Eventually," Norris concluded, "the S.E.C. may regret the steps it is now taking. It is to be hoped that the markets will not have been irreparably harmed in the meantime."[8]

CHAPTER 2

Making the Machine Run

The market is mostly a matter of psychology and emotion,
and all that you find in balance sheets is what you read
into them; we're all guessers to one extent or another, and
when we guess wrong they say we're crooks.
—Major L. L. B. Angas, courtesy of Laszlo Birinyi, Jr.

The New York Stock Exchange, as reorganized by Franklin Roosevelt's New Deal, was an auction market to which brokers who were members of the exchange brought both buy and sell orders from their clients across the country. Of the 1,375 members of the exchange, about 900 worked in the turn-of-the-century grandiose building on Broad Street, 325 of them as brokers carrying orders to the market. "Specialists"—about 350 of them, assigned by the exchange to be the fulcrum of trading in the stocks that were their assignment—stood beside the dozen horseshoe-shaped "posts" on "the floor" in the magnificent seven-story-high trading room. A great gold curtain covered the windows on the Broad Street side to keep out the sun that rose over the Morgan Bank building across the street. The specialists monitored the flow of public business and turned many orders into actual trades, supplying bids for people who wanted to sell and offers for people who wanted to buy if there were no public bids or offers when an order arrived.[1]

Only orders for one hundred shares or some multiple of one hundred shares ("round lots") participated in the auction. Orders for less than one hundred shares, for "odd lots," went to one of about one hundred or so odd-lot brokers, who worked for one of two firms that dealt only in odd lots. These firms simply filled customer orders, buying for or selling from their own firm's account at the next price in the auction, cushioned against price movements by commissions of 12½¢ per share on shares selling for less than $40, 25¢ per share on more expensive merchandise. Bids, offers, and prices were all calibrated in movements of one-eighth of a point. Of the not-quite two million shares traded on an average day in 1950, about two hundred thousand were in odd lots. If someone wanted to buy or (more commonly) sell 150 shares, the fifty piece had to be given to the odd-lot broker.

In principle, "market" orders—orders to buy or sell one hundred shares at the market price at this moment—were always filled, unless the orders on one side were so overwhelmingly large that the specialist felt he had to suspend trading, an action he could take only with the consent of a governor of the exchange. "Limit" orders to sell at prices higher than the market, or to buy at prices lower than the market, would be held by the specialist in his "book," and would be executed by him (for a commission per share roughly equal to that of the odd-lot broker) if and when price changes brought them into line with current bids or offers, thus converting them to "market" orders. When business was slow, as it often was, brokers might hang around the post with a limit order, hoping the price would move enough to get it filled, rather than pay the specialist a commission for executing it. In return for the privilege of the book and the value of being the ultimate market insider, the specialist pledged "to maintain an orderly market" in the stocks assigned to him, selling when there was a scarcity of sell orders, buying when there was a scarcity of buy orders.

Some orders were in effect only at the moment of their entry, some were *Good ToDay,* some *Good Till Cancelled.* To execute trading strategies, customers could enter orders to sell for less or buy for more than the going price ("stop" orders, to stop losses on misguided purchases as a stock declined or on "short sales" as it rose). At least in theory, and mostly in practice, public orders always took priority: The specialist was not allowed to buy or sell at a given price until all public orders at that price had been satisfied.

Trading occurred within a "crowd" assembled at the post. No rule of first come-first served could be followed, because each trade in the auction cleared the floor at that moment. There was a rule that "size takes priority," which meant that any order on the floor large enough to absorb an incoming order on the other side, in its entirety, would be executed before smaller orders. If the total of orders on one side at "the market" was greater than the total on the other side, various results could occur. The specialist might make up the shortfall for his own account, righting the imbalance and keeping the price level, or he might let the members of the crowd "participate" the orders on the heavier side so that some were filled at the current bid (or asked) and some were held waiting the arrival of new offers (or bids). At that point, the price would begin to move, as prices should, in the direction in which the orders were pushing it.

With 10,000 to buy "at the market" and 10,000 to sell "at the market" when the bid was $40 a share and the offer was $40\frac{1}{4}$, the sale occurred at $40\frac{1}{8}$. With 10,000 to buy at the market and only 2,000 to sell, the sale would probably happen at $40\frac{1}{4}$, and the offer would quickly move to $40\frac{3}{8}$, then to $40\frac{1}{2}$, and onward and upward until enough sellers came forth to meet the buyers at the new "market price." At a time when the market was moving very fast, prices could fall or rise through limits and stops on the specialist's book. Though orders were time-stamped when received, and trades were time-stamped as they went onto the "ticker" that recorded them for all the world to see, customers did not have a right to get their market orders executed at the price of trades at the time the order was entered. Each sale ended one auction and started another.

In 1951, when I first visited the exchange, everything associated with trading stocks was a manual operation. The customer's contact into the market was a "customer's man," officially a "registered representative." The customer's man sat somewhere in an office with a telephone. In 1951, his desk was usually in a bullpen, so all the customer's men could see the numbers on the crawl of moving lights or the elongated screen that hung across the front of the room, carrying the news of what had just sold at what price. Often enough, this was a ground floor public space, with customers sitting in armchairs behind a railing that separated them from the brokers, watching the same crawl of lights. Today, of course, the customer's men sit at screens, almost always in cubicles or small rooms rather than in a bullpen, and the public stays home: Few brokers find it good business to pay for retail space.

Much of the buying and selling the customers did was and is on recommendation from the customer's man, who was paid by the brokerage house on the basis of a drawing account against his share of the commissions his customers paid the house. Commissions were high, with the minimum, set by the exchange (nobody could be a member of the exchange who did not agree to charge the minimum commission schedule), running something more than one-half of 1 percent of the price paid (or received) on a sale. For example, one hundred shares at $50, a $5,000 transaction, would cost perhaps $30, on the way in and again on the way out. (By the late 1960s, at the cusp of the movement to put an end to fixed minimum commissions, these fees had risen to very close to a full 1 percent of the price paid for the security.) Of this, the customer's man probably got between $12 and $15. (All these numbers should be multiplied by seven to give their 1992 equivalent.) Even more important to the way the markets worked in the 1950s and 1960s was the fact that commission was calculated per 100 shares: no volume discounts. A thousand-share purchase cost the customer ten times as much commission as a hundred-share purchase.

When he founded Merrill Lynch in 1940, Charles Merrill made much of the fact that his house would pay registered representatives a salary, and would never give them extra commissions because they had customers whose more frequent trading made more money for the firm. He was not tempted to award these registered representatives special bonuses or prizes when they sold securities Merrill Lynch was underwriting, because at the beginning Merrill did not underwrite or distribute securities: It was strictly a broker serving public customers. The few investment houses that lived on trading rather than commissions might have similar attitudes toward compensation. As late as the 1970s, for example, Salomon Brothers established each partner's share of the firm's total profits at the start of the year and did not compensate people according to how much money their activities yielded the company in that year. In both cases, however, there was an annual review, and those who had made it big the year before received a substantial increase in their share of the profits for the next year. Which was not in any way unreasonable.

As the customer's man took the customer's order he wrote a "ticket" describing it, a scribbled notation with the stock symbol and the number of shares on a piece of paper from a two-by-three-inch pad. He called the order to his firm's order department, which sent it down to the floor, where clerks manning telephones in small cubicles against the wall wrote tickets themselves. Half a dozen large firms had "floor members" working every post, and telephone cubicles convenient to every post. Every few minutes, a firm's "floor member" would come by the booth to pick up the tickets from the telephone clerk, who was not permitted to go onto the floor.

Only members were permitted to execute transactions on the floor: If a firm wanted one of its employees to become a broker executing orders, it bought him a "seat." In 1950, a seat cost about fifty thousand dollars. Lesser firms had arrangements to have their orders executed by one or more of the 150 or so free-lance members, "$2 brokers," so named because their commission for executing a trade on behalf of another broker had traditionally been $2 per hundred shares (by 1951, the payment was more commonly $2.50). Brokerage firms with members on the floor also hired $2 brokers, especially on busy days, to cover posts inconvenient to the posts where they usually worked.

If the message for the member was urgent, or if there was business from the phone for a $2 broker, the clerk could use an "annunciator board" system high up in two corners of the trading room. By pushing a button by the phone, he could post on the board a small panel bearing the number of the member he wished to reach, and slap it back and forth, making a flat clapping noise, to improve the chance that the person sought would look up at the board.

Every broker wore a badge with his number. When two brokers completed a trade, they noted down in the hieroglyphics of their work the name of the stock, the number of shares, the price, and the number of the broker on the other side of the transaction.

Meanwhile, a clerk employed by the exchange to do just this and nothing else made up his own notice of the transaction and slipped it into a pneumatic tube that led under the floor and up through the walls to a central unit. Here the exchange's female employees (women were not permitted to work on the floor itself—no ladies' room, you know) keyed the news into the electromechanical system that printed quantities and prices onto long reels of paper in ticker-tape machines all over the country. Part of the brokers' duties was to make sure the specialists and the exchange clerks knew everything about every trade.

The floor members then told their telephone clerks (or gave to a runner to take back to the telephone clerks) the news that the order had been executed, the telephone clerks called the order department, the order department called the customer's men, the customer's men called the customers, and entered the tickets as executed orders to be processed by the "cage" in the "back office." At Merrill Lynch, where everything was entirely up to date in 1951, there were conveyor belts in bands of five that rolled through the office at desk level to carry such tickets to the relevant departments; the keypunch operators in those departments placed stoppers on the belt to hold the tickets in place till they were ready to register the data from them into the Hollerith holes of an old-fashioned stiff IBM card.

At the exchange at the end of the day, the clerks on the floor assembled the tickets and put them into the hands of the exchange's stock-clearing operation, where other clerks worked through the evening matching the brokers' reports of purchases and sales. What matched went forward to "clearance"; what didn't match went back to the brokers who had filed the slips, with instructions to work out the "discrepancies." Most commonly, these were cases where brokers who were sellers had carelessly written that they were the buyers (or vice versa), but disagreements could crop up on price, quantity, or even the stock in question (scores of different stocks being traded at most of the posts). There was plenty of time to resolve these issues, because payment did not have to be made, or securities delivered against the payment, until the fifth day after the trade. There was also plenty of incentive to resolve them fairly, because men who routinely sought to profit by their own errors or the errors of others would find themselves at a disadvantage in the crowd around the specialist's post.

On the fifth day after the trade—"T+5," in the lingo of the business—the securities would be delivered from seller's broker to buyer's broker, who would in turn pass them on to the "transfer agent," usually a bank trust department, which would cancel the registered ownership of the seller and issue new shares of stock to the buyer. In fact, the average time elapsed between a customer's order to sell his stock and the delivery of the certificates to the broker was eight days, which meant a lot of stock had to be borrowed to make on-time deliveries to the purchasers. Immense frames where a single signature was mechanically duplicated on as many as sixty-four certificates at a time allowed whoever was authorized to validate stock certificates to sign his name simultaneously on sixty-four dotted lines.

Those who wanted to buy "on margin"—that is, to borrow some of the purchase price of the stock from the broker—had to keep their shares in "street name" (the broker's name), and give the broker authorization to lend them to people who wanted to "sell short," sell stock they didn't own, and who needed a source of borrowed shares so they could deliver what they had sold. Thus not all the stock sold made the trek to the transfer agent. For some considerable proportion of the total, the transfer was made strictly on the books of the brokerage house holding the shares in its name for the benefit of its customers. Customers were well advised to keep the confirmation records of their trades, which all brokers mailed out, to guard against snafus at the broker's. They still are, though computerized records are much more easily reconstructed than paper records, and everybody has backup files inside Iron Mountain.

Commission payments by customers who bought and sold stock through the brokerage houses accounted for something like three-quarters of the total income of these houses in 1951. Most of the rest was earned through interest on "free balances" in customer accounts (mostly money from sales of stock not yet reinvested: The brokerage houses said they couldn't legally pay their customers interest on that money, because paying interest was something banks did and they were barred from the banking business by law). Another chunk of brokers' income was earned through interest paid the broker by a customer buying on margin, which, for some reason buried in the bowels of history, was not regarded as banking. Yet another piece was earned by the fees customers who sold short paid to borrow the stock they needed to complete their sales. The shibboleth was that commissions paid the costs, and other revenues were all profit.

Floor members in 1951 were permitted to trade for their own account. About twenty of them were full-time traders who did no business with the public, and many more were part-time traders who executed public orders in some stocks and played the market themselves in others. Floor traders were privileged with much information from their presence on the floor, but accepted no specialist's responsibility to maintain an orderly market. Typically, they played very short-term swings in prices. (So did some of the specialists. One of them said to me in 1951, "This job is a ticket on a trolley car. When I feel the trolley car starting up I get aboard; when I feel it slowing down, I get off."[2] This was particularly disturbing from a specialist, who knew because of his book precisely where the trolley stops were.) Other members might mix some trading for their own account with their work as brokers executing orders for their customers, sometimes even in the same stocks. As many as three hundred members were registered with the exchange as at least occasional floor traders until in 1964 the rules made such activity more difficult to carry forward, but it was considered shoddy practice, and it was certainly contrary to the intent of the Securities and Exchange Act of 1934.

Forty Years Later

In 1991, the New York Stock Exchange, though still in the same building and using the same trading floor, would scarcely have been recognized by a Rip Van Winkle who had not seen it for forty years. Physically, it no longer mattered how high the ceiling was above the main trading floor, because a forest of computer screens cantilevered from the posts virtually covered all the walkways between them. (And between the tops of the screens and the still ornate ceiling was a vast assemblage of thick pipes, like the infrastructure of an oil refinery, carrying wires and fiberoptic cables to the posts and their computers.) There were only five much enlarged posts on the main floor and the booths for the clerks had extended well into the room, like the wings of a theater stage. Two other adjacent rooms had been opened, low-ceilinged, blue-walled, and dark, made colorful by computer screens.

Though some specialists still had long narrow "books" hanging from hooks on pillars at the post, most used screens that revealed to them, and sometimes to the brokers in the crowd, the orders to be executed at prices near the current price. On other screens, thrust forward at the post, the specialists displayed the current bid and asked at the post and the size (the number of shares) for which their own market-maker bid and offer were good. The size was measured in round lots—"100" meant 10,000 shares. Another screen showed the bid and asked at any other stock exchanges that traded this stock, via an Intermarket Trading System (ITS), mandated by the Securities and Exchange Commission (SEC) under directives from Congress in the 1970s. With few exceptions, the specialists at the other exchanges whose prices were quoted on the ITS were bidding and offering at those prices for only a few hundred shares. Several NYSE specialists had bold numbers like "1,000" on the screen to indicate that they were prepared to take or sell 100,000 shares of this stock at the quotes posted.

All the odd-lot brokers are gone from the floor now, as are the odd-lot firms. Rather than see the price of their stock rise to numbers that might discourage individual purchasers, corporations over the years typically "split" their stock, giving holders two shares for one as of a certain date. Thus the average price per share held relatively steady from decade to decade, though the averages that measure the movement of the market were up over forty years by roughly an order of magnitude. In constant dollars, a round-lot order in 1991 was about the same as an order for sixteen shares at that price in 1951. Except in the case of a handful of high-priced stocks, therefore, the hundred-share round-lot unit was no longer a barrier to any but the very smallest investors.

By 1991, not only odd lots but medium-sized orders from individual customers were processed electronically. Market orders to buy or sell less than 2,100 shares of a stock (three-quarters of all the orders, though only about a quarter of total daily volume) came over the wires to the post untouched by human hand on the improved Designated Order Turnaround system, otherwise known as SuperDot. The specialist placed the order in the crowd, and if nobody took it within two minutes his clerk executed it for the specialist's own account, at his own bid or asked. The computer printed the trade on what is still called "the tape," though ticker tape and the ingenious machine that was one of the first inventions of Thomas Alva Edison have long gone from the world. What prints on the tape as a transaction is the seller's side. Twenty thousand shares bought by one purchaser from five different sellers will print as five different transactions; twenty thousand shares sold by one seller to five purchasers will print as one transaction.

For orders that make it through telephones to clerks to floor members for execution, the back-and-forth of trading has not changed greatly. The brokers still write tickets and exchange them, reconciliation is still the next morning, settlement is still at T+5. (Various distinguished, learned, and influential committees have decided that securities trades all over the world should be settled on T+3, and the change will come, perhaps soon.) Because such a high proportion of the stocks traded are now registered in "book entry" form rather than held in the form of paper certificates (dematerialized is the term of art), the old problem of getting delivery on time has been reduced if not eliminated. Merrill Lynch has given the process a push by charging a fee to customers who insist on receiving a stock certificate. But very much more merchandise now moves through the auction. The two million shares a day of 1950 have grown to something more than 150 million on average (almost 190 million in the boom-and-bust year of 1987). Memberships that sold for $50,000 in 1950 got to $1.15 million in 1987, and were still near $400,000 in fall 1991.

In 1950, member firms were all individuals or partners. They could not be corporations, because it was considered bad policy to limit the liability of stockbrokers. In theory, however, a stockholder-owned securities firm could be much more richly capitalized than a firm that relied entirely on the resources of its partners. In 1969, the three young turks of Donaldson, Lufkin &

Jenrette (all still under forty) became the first corporately organized member firm, selling 10 percent of their company to the public for $24 million, money that was kept in the firm for capital. Apart from the capital question, many brokers wanted corporate charters for tax reasons and for the personal protection offered by limited liability. In 1971, Merrill Lynch legitimated the idea, and soon thereafter most of the larger houses incorporated.

By 1991, all but a handful of member firms at the New York Stock Exchange had made themselves corporations of one sort or another. Once corporate office was available, the leaders of these firms became less interested in the hurly-burly, not very dignified life of the exchange member working on the floor. A nice symbol of that lack of dignity is the shoe rack in the cloak room of the New York Stock Exchange Club that occupies the seventh floor of the exchange building. Members leave their good shoes at the club and slip into something comfortable for the day's work. (There are also some younger members who leave their running shoes at the club and slip into something more businesslike.)

By 1991, fewer than half the brokers executing trades on the floor of the exchange were members of the exchange. The rest were men and women who rented their seats, usually on an annual basis. The most common year's rent in 1991 was the same fifty thousand (nominal) dollars that had been the *price* of a seat forty years earlier, though the real value of the money was only one-sixth as great. The phrase "$2 broker" was still in common use, but most of these lessors were "contract brokers," who signed up by the month with the brokerage houses, and executed for a flat fee, usually $3,500 a month, all the business the houses sent them. At $3,500 a month the contract broker had to have contracts with several firms if he or she (a ladies' room had been installed) was to make a living on the floor. Contracts being nonexclusive, there was no prohibition on the contract broker executing orders (which would clear through one of the larger firms) for independent traders who were not on the floor. With few exceptions, these "contractuals" were zoned, working at only one post and executing orders for a limited number of stocks. Because they were zoned, it was their business to know everything that was going on at this post. A recognized part of their job was to report back to order departments: "Goldman is buying," "Solly is buying." Because there were a number of them at each post, it was only natural for them to share much of the information they received. For institutional traders who hoped to maintain confidentiality about their strategies, who sprinkled orders around to different brokers to avoid the sight of the same character coming to the post for the same stock hour after hour, the contract broker system was a wiretap that could not be excised from the network.

Enter the Institutions

The most important changes in the stock market had transpired far from the floor of the exchange. These changes involved the nature of the customers, the size of their orders, the compensation they offered the brokers, the source of the brokers' income, and the interfacing between the brokerage houses and the customers' world. They can be simply stated and we shall explore their significance through the rest of this book.

In 1950, insurance companies, a few pension funds, and a few mutual funds were buyers (only infrequently sellers) of shares traded on the stock exchanges. They were already major factors in U.S. capital markets, controlling $107 billion of the nation's $500 billion of financial assets. But they held only $11.6 billion, or 8.1 percent, of the market value of common stock. They understood that if they wished to invest in equities they had to build their positions slowly, and expect to hold them long periods of time, because there was no mechanism by which large orders to buy or sell could be processed through the exchange.

By 1950, the New York Stock Exchange was working on the procedures for "secondary offerings," by which a broker representing a large seller could advertise a "block" of stock to other brokers without actually selling it, until enough buying interest was developed to permit the offering broker, with the cooperation of the specialist in the stock, to place the whole of an unusually large sell order with a number of different customers. The block would then be "crossed" on the floor, usually right after the close, to publicize the transaction. Generally speaking, the seller paid a double commission for such services.

Myron Scholes's Ph.D. dissertation at the University of Chicago looked at the price impact of such large sales in the period 1952–1965, and found that the average price was 2.3 percent below the price of the stock the day before the secondary offering closed. (The decline was most severe, and lasted longest, when the sales were by insiders or by investment companies. Richard A. Brealey of the London Graduate School of Business in 1971 suggested a plausible reason why this would happen: "[I]nvestors correctly guess the identity of the vendor and then react according to the amount of information they believe him to possess."[3]) The same tactics could not be employed to process an unusually large buy order, because sell orders can be shopped to everyone but buy orders can be shopped only to the restricted community that already owns the security. Short sellers, who sold stock they didn't own, borrowing from others to make the delivery, could pick up some of the slack, but the operation was complicated and problematic, because borrowing the stock guaranteed an increased demand later (when it would have to be returned), and those who knew about it could buy with the certainty that there was demand on the horizon. As most institutions have long-term liabilities (the life insurance policy doesn't get paid till the fellow dies, the pension comes up when he retires), the institutions were not terrified by the absence of "liquidity" in their stock portfolios, but the difficulty of getting in and out—and the expense of fixed commissions without volume discounts—unquestionably limited their interest in equity investments.

By 1988, institutional investors controlled more than $6 trillion of the nation's $13 trillion in financial assets, and their $1.3 trillion in corporate equities was 41 percent of the market value of the nation's corporate equities.[4] And many institutions were trading in and out at a rate that turned over their entire portfolio during the course of a single year. The more than one hundred-fold increase in their stockholdings and their dominance of trading activity have been made possible by major changes, behind the continuation of custom on the trading floor, in the way the exchange and its members organize and charge for their services.

In 1951, there were no more than a few dozen trades a year involving as many as ten thousand shares of a company's stock, and these were mostly through the cumbersome "secondary distribution" mechanism. Even in 1965, after the founding of *Institutional Investor* magazine, during the go-go years that John Brooks and "Adam Smith" wrote about, there were only 2,171 such trades a year, less than nine a day, accounting for only 3 percent of the volume on the exchange. But as long as commissions were fixed by the hundred-share round lot, even occasional brokerage of blocks for institutions was incredibly profitable business. Donaldson, Lufkin & Jenrette had been founded in 1959 strictly to serve institutional customers. (In 1991, William Donaldson was chairman of the New York Stock Exchange and Richard Jenrette was CEO of Equitable Insurance.) In 1968, shortly before the first grudging volume discounts came to brokerage on the New York Stock Exchange, a year before he and his partners incorporated their firm, Jenrette told a reporter that "a good idea . . . may be worth $400,000 in brokerage commissions."[5] (One of today's active customer's men comments, "A good idea *is* worth $400,000.")

Though some dealers were resourceful and clever (the 1970–1971 *Institutional Investor Study* by the SEC found some houses that typically increased their holdings to get the price up before disposing of them), block positioning itself "was essentially a loss leader."[6] Prices moved more on the day a block crossed than in the twenty days before or after, and the positioner often had to hold or sell some part of the block at a loss. The *Institutional Investor Study* found that 39 percent of the average block was sold upstairs to institutional investors, 28 percent to other broker/dealers, including both investment houses and specialists, 7 percent to orders in the specialists' books, and 3 percent to individuals. That left 23 percent to be positioned, often enough in circumstances where others in the market knew the block had been incompletely shopped and thus they could safely sell (or buy) against the block positioner. On that 23 percent the average loss was about one-half of 1 percent of the price, but such losses absorbed considerably less than half the high commission paid for trading the block itself. And the willingness to position blocks brought great quantities of hugely profitable additional business.

Some of the extravagant commission money was funneled

around in kickbacks through the "soft dollar" phenomenon, which meant that out of the commissions brokers were glad to buy institutional customers anything they wanted, from research reports to "conferences" in St. Moritz to the services of showgirls. Friends in the brokerage community were rewarded through "give-ups," instructions that commissions on trades executed by X were to be paid to Y. More important, the money was fed back into expanding the business. Led by Salomon Brothers and Goldman, Sachs, many Wall Street firms began to do "block positioning," helping institutional investors sell huge blocks by purchasing the shares themselves, placing themselves at risk that the price would go down before they could dispose of the block. This risk was quite real in the early days, as traders acted on their knowledge that the shelves were heavy with merchandise for sale, but it was nicely cushioned by the high rewards of the commission structure. If a good idea could be worth $400,000 in commissions, a couple of $20,000 losses along the way from positioning securities would not be much of a price to pay for stimulating the business.

These activities could not be quite so conveniently carried on when the institutional investor wished to buy, because the fees for borrowing stock to sell short were subject to negotiation with well-informed lenders. On the other hand, should the positioning house get word from a little birdie that a large buy order was in the works, it could accumulate some stock in advance, pretty much assuring a nice markup (in addition to the commissions) when the order arrived. Much subsequent damage grew from this not-quite-innocent activity of acquiring inventories of stock known to be of interest to institutional buyers. Wilbur Cowett of Wertheim & Co. commented on this favorite new activity on Wall Street: "The dirtiest business I've ever seen, full of wheelers and dealers and chiselers. You never know the real price, because you don't know whether they put it into the commission or not. And even if you could know the real price, it wouldn't help, because you wouldn't know what the side deal was."

By 1985, the number of large block transactions per year had passed the half-million mark, and the 14 billion shares that changed hands in such trades were more than half the total volume of trading that year on the New York Stock Exchange. But the 250-fold growth in volume from 1965 to 1985 was not accompanied by anything like that expansion in commission income for the brokerage houses, because rates on such trading were less than one-tenth what they had been two decades before. After May 1, 1975, on the insistence of the Securities and Exchange Commission, commissions on the exchange became fully negotiable. The real world became one where, more often than not, institutions gave brokerage houses an order and then told them after the trades were completed what they would be paid for their work. Special rewards would be given to brokers who gave an institution "the first call"—that is, tipped off the institution to a recommendation the firm was about to make to the rest of the trade.

With the commission cushion gone, the investment houses had to look at block trading in a different way. Jay Perry of Salomon Brothers said bitterly that "Salomon will no longer be the garbage pail for the world." As institutions did more and more trading, taking positions to facilitate that trading became more and more dangerous. "The principal danger in institutional trading," one trader said, "is getting run over by a Mack truck while you are trying to start your Volkswagen."[7] Using your agent's knowledge for your own benefit became more and more tempting. The opportunity to pre-position what one had reason to believe customers would want became a major reason for continuing in the game.

As late as 1972, SEC Commissioner Philip Loomis could say that "The New York Stock Exchange is a pretty pure agency market," and SEC Chairman William J. Casey could note in passing that 60 percent of the income of the securities industry came in the form of customer commissions. (He was about ten percentage points high, but only ten.) Hurd Baruch of the general counsel's staff at the SEC wrote a bitterly critical book about the broker/dealer firms in 1971, concentrating on their free use of customer balances that totaled more than the capital the owners had in the business, and did not even mention trading by the firms for their own account.[8] The director of compliance for one of the largest firms said in 1974 that "If we find a registered representative buying the same stock his customers are buying at a better price, we can reverse the tickets."

By the first half of 1990, however, according to that year's survey by the Securities Industry Association, commissions accounted for only 16 percent of the revenues of securities firms, and a far smaller share of their profits.[9] The difference was made up in large part by proprietary trading, by firms trading for their own account in the same securities, at the same time, as their customers. Thus, sometimes, inevitably, *against* their customers—that is, the customer, not impossibly on the advice of his broker, is buying the stock his broker is selling. This, too, was not new: It was what the "bucket shops" did in the bad old days before government regulation, and it was a great convenience for a house that had bought the wrong things. The *Special Study* by the SEC in the early 1960s had found that recommending to customers a stock a brokerage house and its partners were eliminating from their own portfolio "is not universally condemned."[10]

Pity the Poor Customer

In 1990, one of the hottest topics in the securities business was the question, "Who owns the customer?" It was being litigated in several courts by lawyers for several brokerage houses and their former "registered representatives." Historically, customer's men moving from one firm to another took their customers with them. That practice has by no means ended, although the standard employment contract for new brokers at many of the securities firms calls for an acknowledgment that customers developed by the broker while employed by the firm "belong" to the firm, and may not be solicited by the broker if he leaves the firm. If the customer wants to follow his broker, however, the contract won't do the house much good. William Power of *The Wall Street Journal* wrote in fall 1990 that major securities houses "are once again going all-out to raid one another's star stock brokers—and their customers. The raiders are dangling recruiting bonuses—called 'bridge compensation'—of $500,000 or more for big-producing brokers willing to jump ship."[11]

Starting with Merrill Lynch in the 1950s, all the major brokerage houses created separate "research departments" to provide recommendations the registered representative could make to his customers. This gave the customer's men tools to promote commissionable purchases or sales (usually purchases), and presumably, if the recommendations paid off, built loyalty to the firm in the breasts of both customer and customer's man. By the 1970s, the firms were all seeking to develop "products" that would *compel* loyalty, because they would be relatively difficult to transfer from one house to another: Individual Retirement Account packages (which securities firms have been known to take six months to move when the customer requests their transfer), Cash Management Accounts, mutual funds owned and operated by the brokerage house, and limited partnerships of various kinds.

Customer's men are paid extra commissions for persuading their customers to buy into these mutual funds and limited partnerships and the selling efforts on limited partnerships, which have the greatest profit for the firm, have often been disgraceful. Prudential-Bache admittedly touted hundreds of millions of dollars into the later all-but-worthless VMS Realty Partners *after* learning that the returns on the properties would not be enough to pay the loans against them. The canned sales pitch read, "Mr. Investor, all you are doing is lending money to a major company that will borrow at established rates, give you a 'floor' of 12 percent for approximately 27 months and give you a share of the upside in real estate that they own or are developing. How much would you like in your account?" Registered representatives were told to pitch the VMS partnerships at "CD and bond buyers" with "pension, IRA and Keogh accounts."[12]

Until the 1980s, the worry about the relationship between customers and their brokers was concentrated on the possibility that the customer's man would "churn" the customer's account, trading him in and out of the market to generate commission income for himself and his firm. In the three-cornered relationship of customer, customer's man, and securities house, the customer's man was the powerful figure. What the firm gave him, essentially, was a place to sit, the use of a telephone, a recognizable name on his calling card, easy access to the trading floors, and billing services. He decided what he would and wouldn't suggest to his customer. If he had low time horizons, and wanted to milk his customers, he could do so. All the "compliance" training given to newcomers at the securities houses, and much of the attention of the "enforcement" people at the exchanges and at the SEC, went to policing the behavior of customer's men when dealing with their customers. Firms were required to file special forms and adopt special monitoring procedures whenever a customer's man had "discretion" over the customer's account (could buy and sell for the customer without the customer's specific approval for each transaction). When the New York Stock Exchange sent its inspectors out to branches of member firms to see how well they were living up to the rules, one of the first things the inspector looked for—I traveled with one of them up to a Connecticut office of Shearson, Hammill one fine fall day twenty years ago, and saw for myself—was the code for monitoring discretionary accounts, and evidence that it was being followed.

All this surveillance was indeed a proper role for a self-regulatory organization, but its psychological effect was to erode everyone's sense that, after all, this was the customer's man's *customer.* There was a real if somewhat unsteady relationship here (always better when the customer's stocks were going up, sometimes awful when the customer's stocks were going down). If the interests of the customer's man were not always and everywhere identical to those of the customer, the latent conflict of interest between the firm and the customer was both more likely to come to the surface and more grave. From the point of view of the executives of the incorporated securities firm, there were always, after all, new customers where this one came from; kids could be hired to work the telephones and recruit them. If there was more money for the firm in selling a customer stock in a new issue, or selling him a municipal bond at a fat markup, or selling him a limited partnership or one of the firm's own "products," the hierarchy of the firm did not necessarily worry about whether this sale was something the customer should do. "Look," said the trader who had persuaded the fledgling Michael Lewis to push some overpriced bonds on a German trader for an Austrian bank, "who do you work for, this guy or Salomon Brothers?"[13]

There is another point of view. "Well," said Donald T. Regan in the 1970s, when he was running Merrill Lynch and his connections with Ronald and Nancy Reagan were still ahead of him, "merchandise does not move unless it's sold. Very few people are self-motivated to go out and buy a book that hasn't been brought to their attention. Bringing our merchandise to people's attention is added effort for our people, so we give them more credit—not more cash in the pocket right now, more credit when salaries are adjusted, twice a year. Our managers are called: 'We have a big issue coming up, it will need pushing.'"

But the customer was the customer's man's lifeline, and it was important to him that his customers made money. "Financial planner" was a term still hidden in the dirty mists of time, but the good customer's man knew the limits of what made sense for his customers. "The cardinal principle laid down by Merrill," Regan added, "is that our people should show our merchandise to our customers, and if the customer says, 'What do you think?' he must be free to say, 'I think there will be a better deal coming along.'" On the other hand, people who moved the more difficult issues, and people who bought them, might qualify for a reward. The most common reward was the chance to get in at the beginning when the firm was underwriting or distributing something hot.

Starting in the 1970s, as the corporate form of organization took over—and with increasing frequency in the 1980s, as corporations that were not securities houses bought these firms (American Express, Sears, Prudential Insurance, Equitable Insurance, General Electric, Home Insurance, Commercial Credit, all acquired brokerage houses)—people who write about financial subjects began to find letters in their mailboxes, sometimes anonymous and sometimes signed, from customer's men complaining that they had been ordered by their supervisors or branch managers to sell their customers what they considered garbage. The men at the desks were increasingly called "salesmen" rather than customer's men or registered representatives. The carrots offered them for executing their orders efficiently were no longer deals advantageous to the customer; they were salesmen's benefits: dinners in the best restaurants, or shows, or even trips for the salesman and his wife, or whomever he wanted to call his wife, to the Bahamas or Hawaii or Paris. Or just a bigger piece of the pie.

By 1991, such behavior had become routine. A story in *The Wall Street Journal* described a memo to Dean Witter branch managers "to push more in-house mutual funds, chiding them for selling too many competing funds that produce less profits for the firm. . . . Brokers typically get paid more to push their own firms' funds. Dean Witter gives brokers 30% to 39% of the sales fee for outside funds, but funnels to brokers 35% to 41% for selling internal funds."[14] Meanwhile, the Dean Witter advertising on television, in black and white, showed a high-collared old-timer telling his salespeople that "We measure success one investor at a time."

As the people who wrote the advertising knew, brokerage is essentially a personal service business. The old partnership forms, with customer's men as associates in the firm, earning a share of the commissions paid by their customers, expressed that personal service relationship. Such relationships were part of what reporter Chris Welles called "the Club," the relatively narrow circle of people admitted to the cozy world of fixed commissions and superior information, which facilitated graciousness and, indeed, honesty.[15] The arrangements were unfair, self-serving, self-righteous, and far from cost-efficient. And they weren't always honest. Some customer's men cheated, abused their influence with their customers, got bees in their bonnets about Real Estate Investment Trusts or commodities straddles or tax-dodging partnerships. Others didn't do their homework or were incompetent at their job, and passed on rumors and bad advice. And some, as is always true in personal service occupations, simply took on too many customers ("one investor at a time," indeed) and didn't deliver to most of them the services for which they were paying. But the great majority of the customer's men were, and to the extent that they can be, still are, protectors of their customers' interests. For the Club had a self-image and most of the members assumed it upon joining.

Incorporation seemed a way to preserve the firms, because partnerships are always endangered by the right of the partners to take their capital when they depart. Modern organization theory approved the concentration of responsibility for the firm's behavior in the hands of its corporate executives, who presumably had less to gain and more to lose from the misbehavior of rogue customer's men. The term "customer's man" acquired a derisory implication. "Registered representative" was more in keeping with egalitarian times. No one worried about the shift of emphasis in the name, from being the outsider's agent to being the insider's employee. "Registration," which implied government approval, was presumed to assure the representative's *bona fides*. But the customer was now really only a customer, and nobody owes fiduciary duties to a customer. In the world of the customer, the rule is always caveat emptor. The stock market ventured into a world of new investment relationships, new technologies, and new academic theories with its ethics totally unprotected.

James Sterngold of *The New York Times* described the attitude of the CEO of E. F. Hutton: "[Robert] Fomon loathed the crass retail trade, which he saw as filled with earnest, half-smart men from the provinces who captained their high school football teams, attended forgettable local colleges, married prom queens, and aspired to little more than honored places on the entertainment committees of their local country clubs. . . . Fomon regarded Hutton's retail customers as sheep waiting to be sheared, and he often said so. He harbored no illusions about the quality of the firm's products. It was the same junk the other firms sold."[16]

As late as the 1970s, academics, regulators, lawyers, and even executives of securities houses were worrying about the conflicts of interest inherent in the underwriting process, when a firm was both promising the corporate issuer the best possible price and promising its brokerage customers a real bargain. By the 1980s, all that was passé, and there was a third party at interest, the house itself, generator of "products," swap contracts, customized derivatives, strips, exotic stuff for sale that almost nobody knew how to price. In 1991, brokers became salesmen for "participations" in bank loans; these participations were not "securities" and thus the 5 percent maximum mark-up rule of the National Association of Securities Dealers did not apply. Suddenly, there was no institutional barrier to pushing the firm's "products" at remarkable markups (Hans-Joerg Rudloff of the London branch of Crédit Suisse–First Boston spoke of bankers who "sold hybrid securities to the public at premiums of 12 and 14 per cent, hiding their profits behind the sophisticated structure of their instruments"[17]); to putting all the information into the computer for the firm's benefit, regardless of the expectations of the customer who made the information available; to reliance on proprietary trading for the bulk of the firm's profits.

In less than a generation, a market where the participants felt themselves protected by an intricate web of fiduciary obligations had passed through the stage of caveat emptor to the Hobbesean condition of *sauve qui peut*. George Gould, who had gone from Donaldson, Lufkin & Jenrette to be James Baker's deputy secretary of the Treasury, then returned to Wall Street to manage about $1.8 billion for the private partnership of Klingenstein & Field, told of a telephone call he had received from a brokerage house that knew he had been investigating the prospects of a medium-sized company traded on the New York Stock Exchange.

"We make relatively large investments in a relatively small number of companies," Gould said, "and everybody knows it. They asked me if I'd be interested in seventy thousand shares, at the market. I said, 'Is it your stock?' [that is, does your firm own it?]. They said, No. I said, 'Is it insider stock?' [that is, are the officers and directors selling out?]. They said, No. I said, 'All right; we'll take it.'

"Later that afternoon, quite by accident, I found out that it *was* insider stock. There was new data about the company since the financials I'd looked at, and it was going to take some big losses. I called the house that had offered it, and I said, 'We're canceling that trade. If you want to complain, you can read about it tomorrow in the *Times*.' They canceled the trade. You know," Gould added thoughtfully, a tall, still graceful man in his sixties with a long, lined, oval face, "they say it's an efficient market. Nobody seems to count the time you have to spend these days looking over your shoulder to make sure there's nobody stabbing you in the back."

CHAPTER 3

The Adversarial Agent

The law locks up the man or woman
Who steals the goose from off the common,
But lets the greater felon loose
Who steals the common from the goose.
> —Eighteenth-century English doggerel condemning the landlords who were fencing in what had been the common lands of the villages

William J. Casey will have fewer footnotes in the history books than he deserves. Very intelligent, very devious, with attitudes formed essentially in the spy business, he was physically repulsive, a fat man with hanging jowls and a belly lopping over his pants, watery eyes and a world-weary manner that virtually ignored the presence of the person whose questions he was answering. A man who had been in some regulatory hot water himself, he was a strange choice by Richard Nixon to head the Securities and Exchange Commission, but in the event—perhaps for the old reason that it takes a thief to catch one—he was one of the most effective chairmen that agency has had. Columbia University law professor William Cary and SEC professional Manuel Cohen had given the agency honest leadership in the Kennedy and Johnson years (Cary gently and Cohen bluntly), but the growth of institutional trading had left the commission far behind conceptually. The agency had run down in Nixon's early days, when an amiable ex-Congressman who liked to be called Judge Budge had yielded primacy in regulation to Nixon's personal friend Bunny Lasker, chairman of the Stock Exchange. Those days happened to coincide with a steep decline in the market and an accelerating collapse of the back offices in the brokerage houses, several of which went bankrupt.

Despite the weaknesses at the exchange, which normally would have been the perfect excuse for inaction (compare for instance, the behavior of the banking regulators in 1990–1991), the SEC under Casey moved ahead on the major issues, restoring capital rules that had been gutted by permissive attitudes at the NYSE, and moving toward the creation of a single national market through electronic linkage of the exchanges. His first act as chairman was to demand a one-third increase in the number of SEC field examiners. It was Casey who bulled through the objections of the industry to order an end to fixed commissions (though he worried about it) and Casey who led the commission through the thicket of the controversy on institutional membership to the imposition of Rule 19b-2. Rule 19b-2 in effect prohibited institutional membership in the exchanges by requiring that brokers holding themselves out as agents for public orders do no more than 20 percent of their business for their own account. The commission defined the problem as "using exchange facilities for private purposes," and proclaimed that "as a central market system develops, it should have at its heart a corps of professional brokers and market makers."[1]

Interviewed in 1973, toward the end of his time on the commission, Casey ruminated about the worst possible future: "The market goes toward trading only in large blocks, and the compensation comes from mark-ups. The values established by institutions throwing blocks back and forth begin to lose credibility." Dealer markets are inherently more unstable than agency markets when the customers are much larger than the dealers. As Charles Bocklett of Weeden & Co., a dealer, put it, remembering his time working for a specialist in IBM, "The players outside the industry are bigger than the players inside. A man makes a decision to take a stand, and he's wrong; another decision, and he's wrong; they come around a third time—he says, I've got to make money on this one or I'm out of business, so he drops the price so far."

The SEC's report on the adoption of Rule 19b-2 quoted a

statement by Thomas G. Corcoran, one of the drafters of the original Securities and Exchange Act, in testimony to the House Committee on Interstate and Foreign Commerce: "The only interest the public has in a stock exchange is that it should be a place where the outside public can buy and sell its stocks. There is no public interest to be served by giving an inside seat to a small group of men who are trading for their own account."[2]

In its original form, the Securities and Exchange Act would have required total segregation of the broker and dealer functions, forbidding those who held themselves out as agents to operate in the market for their own account. "The purpose of this bill," said Colorado Senator Duncan U. Fletcher, "is to insure to the public that the securities exchanges will be fair and open markets. The bill seeks to protect the American people by requiring brokers on these exchanges, members of these exchanges, to be wholly disinterested in performing their services for their clients and for the American people trading on the exchanges."[3] In the end, the question of broker/dealer segregation was referred to the newly formed Securities and Exchange Commission for study and recommendation, and the commissioners decided that "although the combination of the broker and dealer functions did involve serious problems of conflict of interest, there was no need to legislate a complete segregation of these functions inasmuch as we had been granted ample administrative power to deal with most of the known abuses."[4]

In 1945, the SEC Division of Trading and Exchanges, as it was then called, recommended an end to floor trading. "Floor traders," the staff reported, "beyond a doubt enjoy formidable trading advantages over the general public."[5] The commission instead "encouraged" the stock exchanges to promulgate their own rules. These were never such a much, and once the heat was off, the exchanges softened and then dropped the rules.

Following a surprisingly deep but brief collapse of stock prices in 1962, the Congress requested the SEC to perform what came to be called the *Special Study*. This study noted that

Floor members see and hear what is going on and they can react immediately. They know in many instances that a given broker represents certain institutional investors, and may follow his activity closely as he begins to buy or sell large amounts of a stock. They appreciate the trading patterns that generally prevail during acquisition or disposition of large blocks of stock. They are familiar with the trading techniques of different brokers or specialists. They may obtain from fellow brokers or traders general or specific evaluations of investor tenor, in terms of limit or stop orders placed, short sales effected, or orders cancelled. . . . [T]he floor trader is the only member of the Exchange who has no special function and undertakes no obligations in relation to the operation of the market as a public institution. In light of the governing statutory scheme of the last 30 years, this fact, in itself, raises a fundamental question of public policy as to the extent to which a public market may be permitted to shelter such private trading activities.[6]

In response, the commission in 1964 compelled the New York and American Stock Exchanges (but not, interestingly, the regional exchanges, an exemption that subsequently sent considerable business their way) to enact a rule forbidding floor members to buy and sell for their own account any security they had bought or sold that day as agent for anyone else. (The rule was later amended to provide a two-hour "time strike" instead of an all-day prohibition.) Other rules adopted by the exchanges in response to commission pressure gave public orders priority on the floor not only against specialists but also against any member trading for his own account. But the rules applied only to the floor member on the floor: Members and firms were permitted to take positions for themselves in securities their customers traded, provided they did so from upstairs offices rather than on the trading floor.

This had predictable results. To quote a 1967 study for the SEC that the commission did not make public until 1973:

[F]loor trading in relation to total volume declined sharply on the New York exchanges and trading by members off the floor showed a decided increase. This increase reflected not only the fact that some floor traders gave up their floor activities completely and traded exclusively from off the floor, but also the fact that registered traders combined off-floor transactions with on-floor activities since the latter were sharply restricted.[7]

In 1960, New York Stock Exchange member firms that bought and sold shares for their own account did about 57 percent of such business from upstairs offices; by 1989 they did 99.9 percent of their "proprietary trading" upstairs. And trading by nonspecialist member firms for their own account had risen from about 7.5 percent of volume in 1960 to about 15 percent of volume in 1989, which meant that member firms (including specialists) were on one side or the other of about two-fifths of the trades.

Casey noted in 1974 that the commission had gone to Congress for additional powers to curb upstairs trading. Congress did nothing, which does not by any means imply that the SEC lacks power—if anything, the implication is that Congress thought the commission could deal with these matters under its existing authority. Section 11(a) originally ordered the SEC (it was "shall," not "may") to "prescribe such rules and regulations as it deems necessary or appropriate in the public interest or for the protection of investors . . . to prevent such excessive trading on the exchange but off the floor by members, directly or indirectly for their own account, as the commission may deem detrimental to the maintenance of a fair and orderly market."[8]

The 1975 amendments to the act eliminated the term "excessive trading" and instead made it *unlawful* for "any member of a national securities exchange to effect any transaction on such exchange for its own account"—with a list of exceptions that includes almost everything (except, interestingly, trading by a firm that does not "normally" get most of its "gross income" from underwriting or selling securities issued by others, or acting as a broker). The supposed prohibition is then further vitiated in subsection H of the new Section 11(a), which gives the commission power to make whatever other exemptions it wishes to make.

No commission has in fact acted to discipline off-floor trading under Section 11(a) or to compel the exchanges to establish their own rules. If anything, most commissioners since 1975 have wished to *encourage* proprietary trading. Even if they cast a doubting eye on such goings-on, most commissioners seem to believe they lack the authority to do anything about it. Roberta Karmel, who was a commissioner in the Carter and early Reagan days and is now a partner in the law firm of Kelley Drye, says that

"Securities laws don't address the time and place advantage of the upstairs people. The laws have to be rewritten." The only disincentive to taking advantage of special information upstairs is NYSE Rule 390, which requires members to expose all orders on the floor before executing them, and the SEC always has a member or two, Democratic liberal or Republican libertarian, who questions whether Rule 390 is not really a restraint on trade.

In any event, Rule 390 restricts the member firms *only during the trading day*. Between four in the afternoon and nine-thirty the next morning, member firms can buy and sell wherever they can find counterparties, and they don't have to "print" (publicize) the trades unless they wish to do so. Nonmember firms like over-the-counter dealers or London or Tokyo brokers have always been entirely free to deal in NYSE listed stocks without telling the public of their trades. London firms that are not licensed to do business in the United States can trade U.S. securities, as an NYSE broker puts it, "in a closet with the door closed." Weeden's Bocklett, condemning by inference some very large companies, says that "the legitimate investor is reluctant to put his money in London because there's no tape."

There is reason to believe that a great deal of hidden trading occurs in London. In 1988, the Toronto Stock Exchange sent its director of compliance Donald Unruh, a mustached man with military bearing, to scout the trading of Canadian stocks in the former mother country. The recently formed British Securities and Investments Board (SIB) gave him access to the "blotters," the record books, of British firms that were not registered to do business in Canada.

"We had thought there were about fifteen TSE stocks traded in London," Unruh said on his return. "We found more than two hundred of them. Something like twenty per cent of all the trading in Canadian stocks was going on every day in London, and we had no way to know about it."

The proportions may be all of that in American stocks, too. Unruh gave as his personal opinion that 80 percent of the trading in U.S. stocks in London is for U.S. customers. Neither the NYSE nor the SEC has asked the SIB for the sort of assistance that would permit them to do their own analysis, and it is hard to avoid the suspicion that their reticence reflects the influence of the big American houses that trade on four continents for their own account.

Behold the Impact

John J. Morton is a compact Bostonian who ran the securities end of Dewey Square Investors, the operating end of the trust department at the Bank of Boston. He retired in 1988, after spending some years sounding the alarm at meetings of traders and financial analysts about the morality of the stock market. When he left, he had about fifty people working with him in an open office which was not, however, a trader's bullpen—everybody had his own carpeted space, behind waist-high wooden partitions. Most of his people were specialists in one or another industry group. They managed the bank's common funds, and also invested for the individual beneficiaries of the trusts in the bank's care. Unlike the managers of the big mutual funds and big pension funds, they had accounts for which they acquired small parcels of securities as well as accounts for which they bought in the hundred-thousand-share range. As befit an established trust department in an old bank in a tradition-soaked city, Dewey Square bought and sold for its accounts not by negotiating big deals in private with broker/dealer firms or other institutions but by placing orders with brokers to be executed on the floor of the exchange. Among the things Morton tried to do was monitor the "market impact" of his orders: Did purchases for his accounts drive up the price of the shares they bought, and did sales drive the prices down? And if so, why?

Like any money manager or supervisor of money managers, Morton sat with screens on his desk, one reporting current prices, another displaying the highest bid and the lowest offer for any selected stock, as proclaimed at the post by the specialist. The screen also told observers how many shares were being bid for or offered at those prices. Various services offer these quote screens; the most common is Quotron, which Citicorp acquired as part of its commitment to the information revolution, for a price probably twice what the company is now worth. "The Quotron" is the generic term for such screens, as "Xerox" is the generic term for copiers. All orders to buy or sell for Dewey Square passed over Morton's desk, and he kept his eye especially on those stocks.

"It's almost invariable," Morton said, relaxing briefly in a conference room with glass walls that allowed him to keep an eye on the room outside, "that when our broker brings our bid to the specialist a lot of bids follow behind him. I watch the Quotron, and it goes from two thousand bid, one thousand offered to ten thousand bid, one thousand offered. I have to call in the portfolio manager, because you can't trust him to pull his order. His normal reaction is to feel that others have also found the reasoning that led him to this stock, and he'd better pick up as much as he can as fast as he can. The fact usually is that other brokers on the floor have found out about our order, and they're going with the flow.

"We can find out who the brokers are that are bidding against our broker, and we're big enough customers that I can call this fellow's employer and say, 'I want to know whether you have a customer order for this security, or whether there's a firm order, or whether your man is buying it without an order.' And he'll tell me the truth. If the floor broker is doing it for himself or for some friend who's not his employer, I can pull our order. I keep watching the Quotron. A couple of transactions have been done at rising prices. Now the screen goes ten thousand bid, two thousand offered, eight thousand bid, two thousand offered, until finally the crowd realizes we aren't there any more, and the screen begins to show, two thousand bid, ten thousand offered, one thousand bid, ten thousand offered. The price goes down. We send our order back through a different house, and sometimes we can buy at prices lower than they were when we started."

Robert Kirby of Capital Guardian Research gave *Institutional Investor* a specific in early 1987. The fund had a good profit in Upjohn, and decided to take it, selling a large block. Shortly after the sell order had been given to the broker, Kirby saw the stock slide on heavy volume. "I looked at the trading sheets," Kirby said, "and when I saw whom we had given the order to, I said, *'Damn!'* Coincidence? It happens often enough not to soften suspicions."[9]

Once upon a time brokers were agents; they represented buyers and sellers. At some point in the 1980s the language of the Street changed. Institutions were "the buy side." Brokers were "the sell side." In part this was merely a true representation of what history did to the markets. The California Public Employees Retirement System (CALPERS) has an income that averages $42 million a working day from the earnings on its $68 billion of assets and the contributions of the state and its localities. Clearly, CALPERS must over any period of time be a buyer of stocks, as are the pension fund managers for General Motors and AT&T and IBM. Mutual funds have salesmen beating the bushes all over the country; the sales they make translate quickly to purchases by the funds at the Stock Exchange. Necessarily, the institutions are buyers. And brokerage houses were always specialists in selling: The customer's man's central function was to persuade his customer to buy something.

Institutions presumably had much less need for information services. (When Greta Marshall ran CALPERS, she told her traders not to take telephone calls from brokers. They could wire into the CALPERS computers the list of blocks they were buying or selling, but nobody wanted to talk to them. CALPERS had portfolio managers and researchers who would make the decision about what to buy. "And I want to minimize the chance that they will smoke us out.") They were, in principle, long-term investors buying fundamental values; after all, they had long-term liabilities and legal "prudent man" limitations on their investment activities. In 1986, according to a study by Greenwich Research Associates, institutions paid $3.5 billion in investment management fees.[10] Still, it was very useful to get "the first call," and sometimes flattering, too: "I have a concept I want to talk over with you, because you're the only one of my clients I know will understand it." In addition, in the 1980s the supply of equity securities shrank because stock was steadily being locked up in index funds and other stock was bought back by the companies themselves, either as part of leveraged buy-outs or because management wished to use earnings for that purpose rather than for dividends or for further investment in the business. The institutions needed more than just order-executing help from the community of brokers who are in touch with the holders.

Win Some, Lose Some

"Positioning" having become socially acceptable with the spread of block trading, broker/dealers increasingly guessed what was afoot (in extreme cases, they became "risk arbitrageurs," betting on which stocks would be takeover candidates), and went to the institutions as peddlers of stocks they owned themselves, a fact not always acknowledged. The SEC approved the reporting of trades on a basis which permitted a broker who was taking a position to incorporate the commission he was paid into the price; that is, if the previous sale had been at $50⅛, a broker/dealer might buy 100,000 shares from an institution at 50 with a 25¢-per-share commission, and the trade could print at 50¼, showing the stock on the rise and encouraging others to come buy it. As early as 1974, Robert Birnbaum, then president of the American Stock Exchange, said that "The firms that are making the money are the ones with the dealer business. It puts more pressure on their obligations than anything else. And between the lawyers and the accountants, the concept of fiduciary obligation has eroded, though the laws are still on the books."

During this period, the old minimum commissions disappeared—as they should have. They were unconscionable: In 1968, before the SEC began whittling away at the exchange's minimum commission rules, the commission was $44,000 on 100,000 shares of a $50 stock. Such commissions had become counterproductive for the brokerage community, as over-the-counter dealers set up a "third market" that could do transactions for institutions at lower cost. The *Institutional Investor Study* found that the costs of trading in the third market, commissions and/or dealer markups, ran about one-third of what the New York Stock Exchange houses charged in commission, with no reason to believe that buyer or seller got a worse price. Some ambitious technicians started work on computerized "fourth market" systems called AutEx and Instinet, which for trivial fees would bring potential buyers and sellers together anonymously on the computer, to reveal their identities only after they had made their deal.

In 1970, without the consent of his board, NYSE president Robert Haack threw in the towel on negotiated commissions, but his successor James Needham insisted that without rules to enforce minimum commissions the smaller houses would fail (between January 1973 and mid-year 1974, fifty-four smaller brokerage houses that were members of the New York Stock Exchange *did* fail), and large brokerage houses would abandon their Stock Exchange memberships. Those houses one by one began to disown him—first Lehman, then PaineWebber, then Salomon, and finally Goldman, which had been the most belligerent defender of fixed commissions, all conceded the need for negotiated rates. A spokesman for Salomon Brothers told a Senate hearing in early 1973 that "the great majority within the securities industry now believe that fully negotiated commission rates are either desirable or inevitable."[11] In what would prove to be his last speech to an annual convention of the Securities Industry Association, in Boca Raton in 1972, Casey warned against euphoria about the undoubtedly larger marketplace that would follow the move to negotiated commissions. "Unless the brokerage industry has the guts to properly price the services it provides large investors," Casey said, "there is trouble ahead for your firms, for the market, and for the small investor."[12]

Then came May Day, May 1, 1975, and the rate structure simply collapsed. From forty and fifty cents a share, commissions dropped to thirty, then twenty, then ten, and presently even less. Some of the reduced commissions were simply an expression of reduced costs—the electronic order systems, the Securities Industry Automation Corporation to verify the trades, the automated National Securities Clearing Corporation to clear them, and the Depository Trust Corporation to settle them and conduct the actual transfers of ownership, all took major expense items off the budgets of the brokerage houses. The rise in the size of the average "ticket"—from less than four hundred shares in 1970 to more than two thousand in 1990—meant that per-share commissions could drop by a factor of ten and still leave the brokers at least as well off as they had been in the age of fixed commissions. And there was much, much more business. Greenwich Research Associates estimated a total take by brokers from institutions at $1.1 billion in 1975 and $4 billion ten years later.

On larger trades, commission rates of less than ten cents a share were still very profitable. Richard J. Heckman is a blond, athletic ex-Marine pilot from Vietnam days who established his own business in prosthetic devices and served as deputy director of Jimmy Carter's Small Business Administration (the first businessman to hold that job) before turning to stock brokerage. ("But I'd always wanted to be a stockbroker.") As head of the Prudential-Bache office in Rancho Mirage, near Palm Springs, he is extraordinarily busy and prosperous. He reports there have been days when his clients alone have done as much as 4 percent of all the volume on the New York Stock Exchange. He serves the nation's richest community and he writes large tickets for individual investors. "A guy who's going to trade a hundred thousand shares a day at five cents a share will keep a lot of doors open," he said in 1989. "I'll kill for five cents a share, and I'm one of a thundering herd."

By 1990, however, the big traders, the pension fund managers, bank trust departments, insurance companies, and charitable endowments, were no longer paying five cents a share. In essence, they paid what they felt like paying, and often enough, especially on orders for 50,000 shares or more, that could get down to two cents a share, sometimes even less. David Shields is a gracious, handsome man in his forties who with his brother has built a large NYSE floor brokerage business by carefully working large orders on the floor for institutional traders. "Why," he asks, "have we become an industry that lets our customers tell us what we're going to charge? These companies should all take their legal work to Jacoby & Myers."

It was indeed the lawyers who set up this ultimate conflict between the institutions and their brokers. The year before the Stock Exchange moved to negotiated commissions, Congress passed ERISA, the Employee Retirement Income Security Act, which among other things required pension funds to see to it that all their expenditures went to activities that benefitted the people in the pension plan. For reasons that are not clear in any of the associated documents, the law split supervision of pension fund investing between the Labor Department and the SEC. As either could regulate, the lawyers for the institutions decided that their clients could not safely rely on the regulations or opinion letters promulgated (slowly) by either. True safety in buying or selling securities, then, lay not in getting the best advice or the best execution of orders but in paying the lowest commissions. Jack Morton was more than a little disingenuous when he told the National Association of Plan Sponsors in 1987 that it wasn't the institutions that had driven down the rates, it was the brokerage houses competing with each other. They competed with each other because the lawyers for the institutions were telling their clients that brokers were vendors, and under the terms of the law managers would be well advised to buy from the lowest bidder.

"If they want to pay me eight cents a share," said a senior partner in a large firm, "I'll be their agent. If they want to pay me two cents a share, they'll take their chances in the market." As a matter of economic theory, what has happened here is that the institution has suffered an information loss and the broker by becoming a dealer has secured an information gain.

In 1987, even before the market collapse soured everybody, the "Traderforum" division of *Institutional Investor* did "A Survey of U.S. Heads of Equity Trading at Financial Institutions," including both "buyside" and "sellside" traders. About 140 of 545 questionnaires were returned. Almost everyone said that the relationship between the two had changed, and about 70 percent of the traders "agreed partially or fully that the relationship of the sellside to the buyside has become 'intrinsically adversarial' since brokerage firms began taking principal positions in the market." Both buyside and sellside agreed that the worst problems were with "the large mainstream brokerage firms."

If the institutional customers were indeed being traded against by professionals with market inside information, the evidence would be in the "market impact" of their orders and in the results they gained by trading. This is, after all, a zero-sum game. Most stocks will trade during the course of an ordinary day within a range of about 1 percent of their average price for that day. Half the buyers are lucky enough to buy in the lower half of the range and half are unlucky enough to buy in the upper half of the range, and ditto in reverse for the sellers. The real cost of a trade is the commission plus the price by comparison with other prices that day. The market moves in $12\frac{1}{2}$¢ ticks. Saving three cents in commission but buying an eighth up is a mug's game. Pension plan sponsors, a PaineWebber report noted in early 1988, "are beginning to realize that the one, two or three cent trades really may not be the final cost of the transaction." On the other hand, paying three cents more in commission and still buying in the top half of the range or selling in the bottom half will be an even worse bargain for the beneficiaries of the fund doing the trading.

This is where the information loss is felt. The PaineWebber summary of buyside concerns notes the buyside trader's feeling that "day in, day out there are six potential buyers or sellers for every real order appearing on the floor of our exchanges." Dewey Square's Morton had a collection of letters from floor traders and specialists, telling stories of bids or offers that make sense only on the assumption that the bidder knows what's about to come to the post:

It was late in the day in a relatively calm market that was slowly drifting lower. Out of the blue, a broker rushes in to buy 10,000 at the market. He gives up [the name of a firm], which never had a legitimate 10,000 share market order in its life (the term give up means that he is buying it on behalf of that firm, and the sale is to be recorded as one made to the firm), and he says, "There must be some news out there because the guy said to get right out there and buy the stock quick." He is followed immediately by [another broker] who clears for some pretty tricky accounts, bidding the last sale for 20,000.

The next guy in is the broker who, for the first time in three or four days, has the company buy-back order! He proceeds to take it up a half and cross 40,000 [that is, he has both the buyer and seller for 40,000 shares at a price half a point higher than what the market was before this sale]. A blind man can see what has happened and I'm livid. My first thought is to call the company with whom I'm very close and tell them what happened. If I do that, however, [the firm with the buy-back order] doesn't see the company order for ten years.

Instead, I waited until after the close and called a friend [who worked upstairs in the brokerage house that had handled the company order]. I told him the story and said that there was no question that somebody on his desk was tipping his orders. He told me he would look into it.

The next day the broker came into the crowd and said, [the upstairs friend] says to tell you that situation has been taken care of, and that you would know what he meant.

In this case, the leak had come from an order clerk in an upstairs office. More frequently, it comes through the $2 brokers with the rented seats. Another specialist sent Morton another letter, with two cases. One of them described a member firm coming to the specialist and asking what the offer side looked like for a possible buyer. Five minutes later, an options firm that had been offering 10,000 at 54, and knew from the specialist that there was another 40,000 available at that price, canceled its sell order and bought the 40,000. And five minutes after that, the original member firm returned and crossed (that is, effected a transaction all by itself, representing both the buyer and the seller) 150,000 shares at 54¼. Fifty thousand of those were bought from the options firm, which made a very quick $12,500.

Some of the leaks are inevitable if a broker who has been given a large block to buy or sell "shops" his order around to other brokers before trying to work the purchases or sales on the floor. The tension on the floor between brokers and specialists often results from their distrust of each other in situations when there are big orders about to come through. Specialists know which brokers will come to the post with 25,000 shares, sell them, and then reappear the next day with 25,000 more, and (still unadvertised) 25,000 more than that, driving down the value of the specialist's inventory. They also have a sense of which floor brokers are leaking orders to others, cheating the specialist as well as the customer who entered the order.

On the other side, brokers detest the specialists who have learned about a block on the market and use their inside information to position themselves to profit by the institutional trade. The regional exchanges in Chicago, San Francisco, and Philadelphia that trade stocks also listed on the New York Stock Exchange sometimes get business from brokers who wish to make sure the New York specialist for this stock doesn't hold them up. Obviously, the lower the trading volume in a stock, the more help all the participants on the floor must give each other to prevent drastic price changes when there are big orders. Sometimes they give it, and sometimes they don't.

Broker/dealers almost never frontrun their own customers. Perhaps the only exception is when the customer is another division of the same firm, for within today's investment houses all's fair. The most striking example of frontrunning your own orders came at Morgan Stanley in 1988, the *annus mirabilis* of that firm's high-tech trading strategies office and its inventor Nunzio Tartaglia. According to *Trading Systems Technology*, a newsletter of the field, the system employed "Sun-3 and Sun-4 servers, Sun-3 diskless workstations and an Alliant FX/mini-supercomputer. The entire trading system prototype is connected by Ethernet and runs within a uniform Berkeley Unix/NFS environment." The trader workstations were connected with the servers for "real-time analysis of market data," which was then hooked into the system's own "communication nodes for order execution."[13] The rocket scientists found they weren't doing *quite* as well as their models had predicted, and their investigation led them to the belief that the Morgan Stanley order department, through which they had previously put their orders, was frontrunning their trades. The division, which was reported to have a quarter of a billion dollars at its disposal for trading, asked management for the right to place its orders through other firms. Management approved.

Usually, however, the audit trail does not lead back to the firm that handled the order that was leaked. Instead, other firms are permitted to learn about the order, and they make the money by trading ahead of it, a favor that will be reciprocated. Such favors can be done by small operations as well as by mainstream firms. Contract brokers and "boutique" operators, most of them former floor brokers, call on the institutional traders every morning to see if there's any activity they plan in which the boutique might be helpful—and then spend the trading day on the telephone, trading information with contractuals and $2 brokers.

Nobody on the outside can find out which brokers are most heavily involved in this sort of activity. The Toronto Stock Exchange includes on its tape the names of the brokerage firms representing the buyer and seller in every transaction on the TSE, but the New York Stock Exchange considers this information privileged and when pressed will say that there's no point in making it public because firms execute so often for each other's accounts that the names on the tickets are meaningless. Members, however—employers of contract brokers—can usually find out who the brokers were on a big trade.

The four leading services supplying data to institutions that wish to measure the market impact of their trades are the pension consulting firm SEI Corporation, brokerage houses Rochdale Securities and Abel/Noser in New York, and the Plexus Group, a research operation in Santa Monica. Stanley Abel, a man with a bon vivant feeling and appearance, worked for more than twenty years as a floor member of the New York Stock Exchange. His partner Eugene Noser was formerly a pension fund manager for a Southern utility. Their methodology grows out of studies by actuary Stephen A. Berkowitz and Dartmouth finance professor Dennis E. Logue, using data from State Street Bank in Boston, which is the largest trustee for mutual funds, and from the Francis Emory Fitch Company, which keeps a computerized record of every trade every day on the NYSE, generating among other things a volume-weighted average price for every share. The data in the Berkowitz-Logue Study were from the first quarter of 1985, and indicated that market impact costs were not very great on average—only about two cents a share—while commission costs were considerably greater at seven cents a share. "Given what we now know about transaction costs," the authors wrote in *The Journal of Finance,* "pushing commission charges down makes a great deal of sense; cutting commission costs does not seem to produce a corresponding increase in market impact costs."[14]

The range of results around the average was very large, however. The seventy-eight brokers who traded more than 200,000 shares a day for their customers ranged in market impact from +11 basis points (that is, the broker more than paid for his commission by purchasing for his clients below the day's average price and selling for them above the day's average price) to [-]70 basis points (transactions with this broker cost the customer seven-tenths of 1 percent of the money he spent, comparing the price he paid with the volume-weighted average in this stock for the day). But when two periods were compared, brokers who were high cost in one were as likely as not to be average or even low cost in the other. The categories were much more stable when the measurement was managers—fund managers whose transactions were expensive in one period tended to have expensive transactions in the others. It is not impossible, though—as we shall see in the last chapter—that they were buying something for that money.

Abel/Noser has developed a service based on the Berkowitz-Logue technique that measures for institutions their full transaction costs, commission plus market impact, for each day. The service is paid for by the allocation of brokerage work, usually at 2¢ a share. ("We can show you two Rolls-Royces in garages down here," says Stanley Abel, "that testify to all the money you can make in this business at two cents a share.") Admiration for Abel/Noser is restrained in most of Wall Street. Laszlo Birinyi, Jr., has criticized the methodology and the shallowness of the historical data (his computers have all the trades on the NYSE going back to the turn of the century). David Shields observes mildly that if a stock is rising during the course of a day, buy orders placed in the afternoon will seem to show a greater market impact (the price will be higher than the weighted average) than orders placed in the morning. Indeed, the simplest explanation of the Berkowitz-Logue data on the importance of managers to market impact costs may well be that managers who try to ride trends get in a little later than others. And that the funds that get the first call tend to buy or sell at better prices than funds that are not the beneficiaries of such largesse.

Plexus Group, headed by the financial analyst and statistician Wayne Wagner, has a copyright "Alpha Capture" measurement that takes into account the difficulty of the trades as well as commission cost and "impact." Wagner's methods show impact costs almost five times as great as those in the Berkowitz-Logue study, and also find consistent impact cost differences according to the broker employed. "We conclude," said a Plexus document in mid-1990, "that there are significant constituencies with a stake in promoting an illusion or delusion of low transaction costs. The manager who sees through the illusion possesses a powerful tool to outperform other managers entranced with the emperor's new clothes."[15] Wagner specializes in finding off-board ways for institutions to trade with each other without the intervention of brokers, a subject we shall consider in detail in chapter 6. For several years, Plexus was Reuters' manager for The Crossing Network, which permitted institutions to trade with each other at 5:00 in the afternoon Eastern Standard Time, an hour after the close of the New York Stock Exchange, at the closing prices of that day on the exchange.

For most managers, and indeed for most public purposes as Wall Street news is reported, what matters is not the comparison between the price paid today and the volume-weighted average price today but the comparison between the price paid today and the price at the close. Tomorrow's newspaper will report the price of shares in each mutual fund according to the closing price of the stocks in its portfolio today. Anybody from outside who looks at the pension fund portfolio and its changes will compare the prices paid today with the closing prices. And the very cheapest transactions, especially of large "programs" involving the purchase or sale of many different stocks, can be arranged at those closing prices, executed by over-the-counter dealers in Los Angeles or in London. Trading is very heavy in the last few minutes every day, dominated by "MOC" ("Market On Close") orders. And the overwhelming majority of trades in the minutes just before the close occur in the top or bottom 10 percent of that day's price range.

Given the quantity of orders to be executed after the close at the closing price—and the fact that options can be exercised at that price that evening—MOC orders obviously can have manipulative intent, and there is occasional direct evidence that they do. One floor broker tells of another rushing breathlessly to the specialist at three minutes to four with 12,000 shares in a not very active stock. The specialist happened to be heavy with inventory in this stock and said, "Okay. I can do that at the market," and the broker said, "No, no, you don't understand. I'm supposed to buy it sloppy."

It should be noted that except for unreported trading after the close, the closing price has no utility—except, one cynical broker says, that in a market manipulated by arbitrageurs, people can protect their clients by executing some fraction of their orders at the close. It does not predict tomorrow's opening price (indeed, almost as much price movement occurs between today's close and tomorrow's opening as occurs during the trading day), and it does not represent what this stock or this fund was really worth today while the market was open. Brokers executing large orders piecemeal on the floor give clients their average price for all their transactions that day. What the papers should report in pricing mutual funds, and the number the mutual fund managers should give the plan sponsors every night, is the price of the stocks in the portfolio on today's volume-weighted average. That might or might not shrink the abuse of market-on-close orders and aggressive index trading, but it would in any event have the virtue of honesty.

What the Commissions Can Buy

By general agreement, the worst aspect of the fixed commission system had been the "soft dollar" phenomenon. The commissions that had to be paid to execute the trade were so much greater than the broker's costs that he would have been happy to cut his price if the world had let him do so. As the rules were rigid about how much he had to charge, the broker gave the fund manager gifts, as the savings and loans and the banks gave depositors everything from toasters to television sets in the days when the interest rates they could pay were subject to low government ceilings. If the fund manager didn't want a gift for himself, he could direct the broker to favor someone else. "This has had the effect," the SEC letter of transmittal of the *Institutional Investor Study* told the Congress, very politely, "of making commission rates for institutions negotiable but limiting the extent to which the ultimate investor rather than the money manager has benefited from such negotiation."[16]

An article in *Institutional Investor* magazine in 1973 described "the soft commission dollar" as "one of modern economic technology's most versatile tools. Its directability, plus the fact that it must be paid to *somebody* at rates that until recently were wholly fixed, ranks it as a lubricant that rivals the best Exxon has to offer. The soft dollar can be squished through channels of infinitely varying diameter and sliced more ways than a Sicilian pizza. Money managers who would not be so gross as to pass a cash bribe under the table to influence a trader might be tempted by commission dollars that must be paid anyway."[17]

The most common abuse was the allocation of dollars that were being paid to execute trades for a mutual fund to the broker/dealers who sold the fund, as an added commission on sales. Next came the demand by banks that "give-ups" be awarded to broker/dealer firms that kept high balances in their checking accounts. It was not unknown for pension "consultants" to approach a brokerage house with suggestions that if presented with a certain percentage of soft dollars they would be happy to recommend this broker to the fund managers. SEC statements began criticizing such practices in 1964, but they were not actually prohibited until 1974.

The most defensible use of soft dollars was to reward firms—brokers or analysts—that had done the research leading to the purchase or sale of the stock. But even this, Salomon's counsel Donald Feuerstein told the Senate in 1973, was undesirable, because "It is impossible to distinguish between brokerage commissions paid for investment research and those paid for other reasons."[18] Feuerstein noted also that others had said that prohibiting brokers from allocating soft dollars to pay for research services

> would result in a substantial segment of the research function being performed by independent firms dedicated to that function rather than by broker/dealers. We would consider that result to be beneficial rather than detrimental. All too often broker/dealer research departments are used merely as sales tools to generate business rather than as sources of disinterested advice. Because it is easier for most brokerage firms to execute buy orders rather than sell orders, and because negative research reports may irritate investment banking clients, buy recommendations are much more common on Wall Street. Hold recommendations are very rare because they result in no business whatsoever. After a large underwriting syndicate has been assembled, there are often few, if any, independent commentators left to give a disinterested appraisal of the new offering.[19]

In those days, of course, Salomon—very much a trading house—did not have an equities research department. Birinyi tells a charming story from his time there of the day when the house positioned a large block of Mesabi Trust, and found out only after they had resold the stock that they had for some hours been major stockholders in a mining company not, as they had thought, a Japanese bank.

Negotiated commissions presumably reduced to something like a vanishing point the money that would be available for soft dollars, and ERISA—the pension reform law—made the legality of such payments questionable by requiring that fund managers seek to recapture any excess commission revenues for the beneficiaries of the pension plan. Scarcely was the ink dry on the legislation, however, than the Securities Industry Association came pleading to the Congress for an amendment that would define expenditures on research as for the benefit of the pensioners. An amendment to the Securities Act created Section 28(e), empowering the SEC to give a "safe harbor" to fund managers who give business to brokers knowing that soft dollars from that business will be available for allocation to third parties.

Under Harold Williams, Jimmy Carter's SEC chairman, this responsibility was taken seriously, and the flow of soft dollars became a trickle. Under John Shad, Ronald Reagan's SEC chairman, the spigots were opened. The SEC defined "research" as any product or service which "provides lawful and appropriate assistance to the money manager's decision-making process." After all, the institutions were big boys; they could police the abuse of soft dollars themselves. You don't have to turn your back for long before a lot of money passes through that definition coupled with that attitude. "People are talking about bribery," says a veteran New York customer's man, "and they use the words 'soft dollars' to cover it."

"I can't tell you," said Pru-Bache's Richard Heckman in Rancho Mirage, "what I've been asked to do with the soft dollars to get the business." The details of what the SEC has done in the soft-dollar area—and the surprising identities of those who denounce it—are matters for chapter 7. For now I note only an encounter at a humongous party given at the Hotel Pierre in New York for some occasion, perhaps the Emperor's birthday, by Yamaichi Securities. Among those present was a man I had last spoken with on the exchange floor, where he was a member for one of the big houses. He'd changed jobs, he said; he'd gone to work in his firm's soft-dollar department. There was much more money to be made in that business.

Club Rules and the Zeitgeist

The danger of writing about these subjects is that the reader will think he is looking into a snake pit. In fact, the vast majority of people who work in the business of trading securities are honorable men well beyond the normal constraints of the goody-goods at the Better Business Bureau. The culture of today's lawyers—the feeling that it's okay to do anything that isn't actually prohibited by law—has not permeated the inner world of the Stock Exchange, which indeed could not function if sanctions for dishonest and destructive behavior within the club could come only after due process. The reflex response to the collapse of commission rates is aberrational, and by 1991—which was a little late but not bad by comparison with the usual business learning curve—the leadership of the exchange was hunting for ways to follow the prescription Casey's SEC wrote when submitting its *Institutional Investor Study* to Congress: "The values of the agency auction market must be preserved."[20]

The task of preserving both agency and auction has been made immensely more difficult by the public ownership of brokerage firms and investment banks, technological advance, academic incomprehension, and the erosion of the sense of fiduciary responsibility in late twentieth-century America. Political leadership especially still has much to learn, and much to answer for.

CHAPTER 4

Living with the Futures

When a woman is poorly dressed you notice the dress. When a woman is impeccably dressed, you notice the woman.
—Coco Chanel, courtesy Laszlo Birinyi, Jr.

Into this slippery-slidey world of lost imperatives came the artificial constructs traded in the Chicago commodities markets. Until the 1970s, these markets—the Chicago Board of Trade and the Chicago Mercantile Exchange—in fact traded only contracts requiring the purchase or delivery of a physical commodity. The essence of the system (which went back only to the mid-1920s, though the Board of Trade was solidly nineteenth century in its foundation) was the creation of two separate instruments at the conclusion of each trade. Instead of having a contract to buy from or deliver to the person on the other side of the transaction, the buyer or seller of a future wound up with an obligation to the "clearing corporation," jointly owned by all the members of the exchange itself. And the counterparty to the trade had his own separate contract with the clearing corporation.

Each contract had an expiration date on which the seller could be forced to deliver a carload of the commodity being traded to a specified delivery point, and the buyer could be forced to accept that delivery at that place. If the contracts were still alive on their expiration date, the clearing corporation would match them on a random basis, then tell each buyer the name of the company that would deliver, and each seller the name of the company that would accept delivery—almost never the same name that had appeared on either side of the original trade. Either party could always extinguish his obligation by purchasing or selling an exactly opposite contract for the same commodity with the same expiration date, and nobody would tell the original counterparty that such a transaction had occurred. For most commodities, nearly all contracts were in fact settled before their expiration by some countervailing trade.

All these contracts had three purposes. First, they allowed producers and users of the commodity to lock in the price at which they sold or bought, some months before the commodity was ready for delivery. It was not necessary to use the contract to buy "the physical," the commodity itself. Even a purchaser who wanted delivery would usually sell the contract at the end and buy separately in the "cash" market, taking profits (or absorbing losses) on the contract that in effect eliminated the change in actual price from the day he acquired it to the day of his real-world purchase or sale. The reason for buying or selling in the cash market was usually that the delivery point specified in the futures contract was too remote for the buyer, who in any event had established delivery arrangements with his usual suppliers.

Second, these contracts satisfied—indeed, sanctified—the gambling propensities of the commodity traders who took the other side of a producer's or user's deal, ensuring that buyers and sellers could always find a liquid market.

Third, the contracts created a standardized unit of account by which different grades of wheat or coffee or potatoes could be traded together. The seller could deliver hard winter wheat or spring wheat or whatever, at an established discount from or premium to the contract price. Prior to the futures contract, one could not really talk about a price for "wheat," only about a bunch of prices for different grades of wheat. This was another reason for players in the futures markets to sell their contracts and buy in the cash market: The futures contract could be satisfied with several different grades of wheat, but if you were making spaghetti you wanted durum semolina and nothing else.

There has always been concern about what futures markets

were doing. Farmers always felt the speculators were driving down their prices, and millers always felt the speculators were pushing up their prices. Because contracts could be created in any quantity but the supply of the commodity was limited, people worried that the market could be "cornered" by someone who bought up a lot of contracts and then squeezed the sellers by demanding delivery.

A lot of contracts could in fact be bought with a very small investment. To make sure the speculators could afford to play, contracts could be bought with down payments that were a few percent of the value of the commodities they controlled. A man might control a million dollars' worth of corn or pork bellies on "margin" of perhaps $40,000. To make sure traders did not welsh on their deals, this margin had to be recalculated every evening. If the trader was long and the price fell 1 percent, he or she would have to put up another $10,000 in margin before the market opened the next day; if it rose 1 percent, he or she could take $10,000 out. If it rose 4 percent, there would be sufficient margin to buy another million-dollar contract. Pyramiding was easy and immensely profitable. A trader who caught onto a trend could quickly make ten times an initial bet—and then lose it all in a few days.

On Wall Street, the successful speculator was the "contrarian," the man who argued that by the time the public knew a story and began buying into a situation, the profit was out of it. Traders watched the odd-lot volume: When the public was selling, it was a good time to buy, and when the public was buying, everyone should head for the hills. Even now, *The New York Times* winsomely prints each week a report on the "put/call" ratio, pointing out that when the number reaches 1.3 (many more purchases of puts than of calls), the signs are bullish; when the number reaches 0.6 (more calls than puts), the bears have it. In Chicago, by contrast, the theory was "the trend is your friend," and the speculator sought to hook onto whatever was fashionable, hoping to get out at the turn. Thus commodity prices spiked higher and lower than stock prices; the good market from the trader's point of view was the one where prices reversed ten times a year; and it could happen. Commodity markets set "limits," maximum price moves for a single day's trading; once those limits had been hit, trading would cease, unless someone wished to buy at a price at or above the limit, if the market had fallen; or sell at or below the limit, if it had risen.

Traders had to keep deposits at the clearing corporation large enough to make the clearing corporation feel secure about taking the counterparty role in their trades. Brokers ("Futures Commission Merchants," or FCMs) had to identify to the clearing corporation the customers who had placed the orders. The clearing corporation kept track of how many contracts each large customer had bought, retaining the right to compel sales if the exchange thought a corner was in process of construction. This right is alive and well: The Board of Trade used it against an Italian trading firm that was buying too many soybeans in 1990. New York's Comex in 1979, at the belated insistence of the Commodities Futures Trading Commission, used a similar ploy, forbidding purchases except by traders liquidating short positions, to frustrate the Hunt brothers' effort to corner silver.[1]

In 1971, an ardent lawyer-turned-trader named Leo Melamed, a small, black-haired man with quick motions and a quick mind, speaking with a trace of the sing-song accents of the Polish *shtettel* though he had come to Chicago before his tenth birthday, persuaded his fellows at the Chicago Mercantile Exchange to begin trading contracts that would require the purchase or delivery of foreign currencies, originally the pound, the French franc, the Swiss franc, the German mark, and the Mexican peso (the last of these died a sudden death). Melamed was then president of the Merc, having led a Young Turk rebellion in the 1960s, and having also (it was the source of his loyal following) redesigned the live cattle contract to make it a much more popular trading vehicle.

The "financial futures" Melamed introduced to the Merc made that formerly rather scruffy institution one of the powers of world finance, eventually the developer (with Reuters) of the computerized Globex system that may well replace trading floors everywhere before the dawn of the next century. In 1968, when Melamed became the youngest president the Merc had ever had, its revenues as an exchange were a derisory six figures a year and it lived in nondescript rented space in a nondescript 1920s office building. In 1991, when he retired from the last of the leadership posts he held with the exchange, the Merc's revenues were in nine figures a year, and it was the proprietor of new twin forty-story towers flanking a triple-decker of trading floors along the Chicago River.

When the currency futures began trading in 1972, interestingly—speaking of regulation and deregulation—the Merc did not need the permission of any government agency to open shop. The Department of Agriculture regulated the introduction and to a degree the trading of futures contracts for agricultural commodities, and that was all the contracts there were. Nobody traded gold futures: Since 1933, the price of gold had been fixed by the United States at $32 an ounce, and although prices might fluctuate around that standard at the London gold "fixings" each morning and afternoon, there wasn't anywhere near enough volatility to tempt traders. Nobody traded oil yet; the Texas Railroad Commission controlled American production to keep prices above $2 a barrel, and the cartel of worldwide oil companies was alive and well in the Persian Gulf.

Like the contracts for wheat or corn or cattle, Melamed's currency futures were usually settled by selling the contracts rather than by delivering the currencies. The purpose of trading foreign exchange in a futures market in Chicago was most commonly to lock in the value of payments that were going to be made by or to Americans in a foreign currency. The contract was a true futures contract of a traditional kind, however, and the buyer always had the right to demand delivery of the "commodity" at its expiration.

Melamed's invention that made this market go—and made some of his friends very rich—was the creation of a cadre of specialized traders who did nothing but arbitrage between the prices the banks were charging for "forward delivery" of foreign currencies and the prices on the futures contracts at the Merc. These traders were never at risk, because they bought from or sold forward positions to the banks at the same time they were selling or buying futures contracts in the "currency pits." Without such arbitrageurs, Melamed pointed out, "we could never have been sure that our prices were the real market." The banks could have done this for their own account (indeed, in the 1980s they learned to do just that and began wiping out the little speculators), but they found the market undignified. Though they refused to participate in the market, they did give Melamed the facilities he needed, because the deposits of the clearing corporations were a significant source of their overnight funds, which was more important than dignity.

Meanwhile, at the Board of Trade, another form of financial future was being developed by a very different man, Richard Sandor, a curly-haired whip-smart young University of California economics professor with a specialty in real estate financing, who was interested in improving the secondary market for the federally insured mortgage instruments issued through the Government National Mortgage Association (GNMA or popularly, Ginnie Mae). These were very complicated self-liquidating "pass-through certificates" which paid their purchasers from the total cash flow of payments by householders—principal and interest—on a large package of mortgages that came due at roughly the same time. When interest rates went up, the pass-throughs paid off more slowly, because people were less likely to sell their old homes with their low-paying mortgages and assume a high-paying mortgage on a new home. When interest rates went down, the pass-throughs paid off more quickly, because people refinanced their loans. Originators of mortgages had good reason to wish to know the rates at which they could offer mortgages to homebuyers in sixty or ninety days, for it took time to close real estate deals. Some investors in mortgages, notably insurance companies and pension funds, received their funds in a rather lumpy fashion, in monthly or quarterly bursts, and had reason to buy instruments that would let them lock in the interest rate they would receive when they got the money to buy.

By the time Sandor's Ginnie Mae futures were ready for trading, Congress had created a Commodity Futures Trading Commission (CFTC) from a rib of the Agriculture Department, and (in part at Melamed and Sandor's urging) had included in its charter the authority to regulate and supervise trading in futures for "tangible and intangible" products. So Sandor needed permission—and got it. The day before trading was to begin, the SEC sued to enjoin the CFTC from approving the contract, on the grounds that it was a "security," and thus within SEC jurisdiction. But the courts, in a decision that still reverberates, decided that a futures contract was *not* a security. The case was made easier by the fact that the SEC did not regulate the issuance of the Ginnie Maes, because securities sold by U.S. government agencies are exempt from regulation or even investigation by any other government agency.

Ginnie Mae futures never got far off the ground, mostly, Sandor later realized, because the cash market for Ginnie Maes was imperfect. Like the wheat contract, the Ginnie Mae future attempted to specify various grades of financial instruments that could be delivered in satisfaction of its terms, but even with the abstract futures contract as a substitute, these certificates were tricky investments for anyone looking to trade the market rather than make long-term investments. Because the cash market was imperfect, the prearranged discounts or premiums for GNMAs of different characteristics could get out of line with the discounts and premiums that were in fact being charged and received. This would drive the price of the futures contract down as the expiration date neared, because the buyers wanted to sell the contract rather than take delivery, and the sellers of contracts wanted to deliver bargain bonds rather than take any profits they might have (let alone losses they had suffered) in the futures markets. One could not mathematically equilibrate a 6 percent mortgage and a 14 percent mortgage, because the latter was much more likely to be paid off ahead of time. Finally, there was no way a trader who was long the futures could hedge his position by shorting the actual bonds, because there was no broker or agency lending bonds for the purpose of short sales.

Sandor looked for another financial instrument that could be the wheat-like commodity for which a futures market might be created, and he found the U.S. Treasury bond. It was the perfect solution. Long-term interest rates on all bonds and mortgages tend to move in the same direction in any period of time. Thus a futures contract for a T-bond would meet the needs of the mortgage originators and investors, and also take care of other people's problems. Underwriters of corporate and municipal bonds, for example, had to price an interest rate for the issuers before they offered the paper to the public. For a brief period between the issue date and the sale, they were at the mercy of interest-rate fluctuations—as, indeed, were the larger customers. By selling a T-bond future, an investment banker underwriting a bond issue could protect himself against a sudden rise in market interest rates.

The intellectual accomplishment represented by this contract has not been sufficiently appreciated. What Sandor did was to construct an abstract U.S. Treasury bond, which carried an 8 percent coupon (that is, it paid interest at 8 percent annually), and ran for thirty years. This abstract bond was traded in the T-bond pit for delivery on a date certain (one such each quarter). This soon became the most active commodity market in the world. If the contract ran to term, it could be satisfied with the delivery of any Treasury bond with at least fifteen years to run. The value of that bond was calculated by reference to its interest rate and the time that would have to elapse before its expiration. A pre-established (mathematically calculable) "conversion factor" equates real bonds to the nominal 8 percent Treasury bond of the futures contract.[2] Putting together a mix of bonds to satisfy the T-bond futures contract was an exercise quite similar to putting together a mix of grades of wheat to satisfy a wheat futures contract. As with the wheat traders, some brokers became especially expert at finding bonds they could buy for a little less than their worth after the conversion factor was applied. Borrowing T-bonds for short-selling purposes was a cinch: Banks and insurance companies were forever lending bonds to each other to facilitate repurchase agreements.

Prior to the development of the futures contract, the cash market in government bonds had traded a "benchmark" bond, that could not be easily arbitraged against bonds that came due in other years and paid different interest rates. Insurance companies were and are the main customers for long-term Treasury paper, and they buy bonds according to what their actuaries tell them they will need to pay off policies that expire in different years. The U.S. government, however, offers bonds according to the money it needs to fund this year's deficits. As there was no necessary correlation between government deficits and what insurance companies would need thirty years later, government bonds due in different years sold at prices that might be well off their proper price with reference to the benchmark. (Japanese government bonds from the "off years" sometimes sold to yield twice what the Japanese benchmark yielded, because the benchmark was in such heavy demand for trading purposes.) Because all bonds with more than fifteen years to run could be arbitraged against the Board of Trade's T-bond contract, their prices solidified around an established differential of the conversion factor. Like other commodity futures contracts, of course, the T-bond contract was normally extinguished by the purchase of a countervailing contract rather than by the delivery of the underlying "commodity."

Sandor's T-bond contract came on stream in mid-1977, and Salomon Brothers used it two years later to protect itself against the prospect that interest rates might spike up (producing a drop in the price of bonds) while the house was marketing IBM's first large bond issue, of which it was a lead underwriter. In fact, Paul Volcker's Saturday night massacre of October 1979, when the Federal Reserve announced an intention to let interest rates soar as the best way to control inflation, did intervene between the registration of these bonds and their sale, and the money Solly made on its T-bond contracts saved the firm from tens of millions of dollars in underwriting losses.

The Cash Settlement Revolution

These financial futures retained the basic characteristic of the agricultural future: It was possible for the buyer to insist on taking delivery, or the seller to insist on making delivery, of the underlying commodity. Then, in 1981, with the Reagan administration in full fig and a new chairperson of the Commodities Futures Trading Corporation looking to enlarge her realm, Melamed and the Merc made a breakthrough, to a Commodities contract that would settle not with the delivery of the commodity, but with a cash payment by the clearing corporation to the winners and from the losers to the clearing corporation.

This was the Eurodollar contract, a contract that priced the interest rate on short-term dollar-denominated Certificates of Deposits in banks or branches outside the United States (almost always in London). This was a very useful instrument, of value to anyone who planned to borrow or lend in an international nexus—or, indeed, domestically, because the rates moved together—in the next ninety days. Both businessmen and bankers could proceed with the assurance that they knew the cost of funds at the time they would need them. Banks had traditionally given forward commitments, but they were expensive, whereas trading Eurodollar CD contracts in a Chicago pit was cheap. The fact that the CDs would be lodged overseas, however, meant that delivery could not be made in the United States. In addition, because the purchasers and sellers of these contracts were trading in million-dollar pieces, only banks or truly giant corporations could play if the holder of the buy contract had the right to force the seller to supply him with the money. Permission was therefore given for cash settlement of the Eurodollar CD contract: Nobody could demand delivery. If interest rates went down in the ninety days, owners of the futures contracts would be entitled to a payment expressing the difference between what they would be paid for lending their money now and what they would have been paid had they made the loan (bought a CD) when they acquired the contract.

Once it was no longer necessary to have a commodity that could be delivered as the basis of a futures contract, once it was legal to trade commodities on a basis of cash settlement, the world was open to all sorts of new instruments. The British bookmaker Ladbroke's had long accepted bets on the movement of the Dow-Jones Industrial Average, the most widely accepted measurement of the performance of the stock market. Jim Cayne, the aggressive president of the Wall Street house Bear Stearns and world-class card player, who had played bridge with Melamed when he was a scrap-iron dealer in Chicago, remembers calling Melamed from London to ask, Why don't you do this on the Merc? Cayne was already late. Melamed had never forgotten conversations he had overheard among the veteran traders at the Merc when he first came to work there as a runner in the 1950s. Their dream contract, they said, the futures instrument that would really bring the public to their market with money in hand, was a contract on the Dow. Melamed had bought into that dream together with the rest of the Merc culture.

Both Chicago exchanges prepared to trade a futures contract on the stock market, the Board of Trade claiming rights to the Dow, and Melamed, unable to compete with the senior market, claiming the Standard & Poor's 500 index, a much broader measurement of market performance. The Dow left out many stocks that were in the S&P 500 and the weightings of the stocks were quite different in the two calculations. Each S&P point was worth about eight Dow points; with the S&P at 300, the Dow would be at roughly 2400. The Board of Trade assumed that the Dow Average, as a published number continuously updated and circulated worldwide, could be used as the basis of a contract without any consent from or payment to Dow-Jones.[3] Melamed took a different view, in part because he needed assured secrecy from S&P to guarantee that insiders could not benefit from disruptions in the price of the index when some stocks were deleted and others added, and in part because he needed respectability. And the S&P was, in fact, a better basis for a contract. Melamed's negotiations with both S&P and the Commodity Futures Trading Commission were arduous and time-consuming. One of the Merc's claims for the S&P as against the Dow in its approach to the CFTC was that the large number of stocks in the S&P would make that index impossible to manipulate by purchase or sale, whereas the thirty-stock Dow might tempt some sure-thing artists to victimize the public.

In the end, the Kansas City exchange got the first approval to trade a contract based on stock prices, as listed in the Value Line Index. The Value Line Index is a strange measurement that takes more than sixteen hundred stocks and measures the percentage movements in the price of each with equal weighting for all. It wasn't a measure most of the trading community was used to, and Kansas City wasn't a place where the securities business had a heavy representation. The Board of Trade was placed hors de combat when Dow-Jones won an injunction prohibiting anyone from trading a contract on its copyright product without its consent. (Eventually, the Board of Trade would invent its own "major market index"—MMI—which tracks twenty stocks, including seventeen in the Dow.) Melamed's S&P 500 contract became, in effect, the only game in town through the formative years of index trading.

As a trading matter, the S&P 500 was a simple contract. Standard & Poor's computers continually tracked the prices of the stocks in the index, weighted them according to the company's capitalization as a percentage of the total capitalization of all 500 stocks, and printed out a number. That number multiplied by 500 was the instantaneous stock market value of the index contract. If the index was at 300, the contract was worth $150,000. A futures contract, however, is a prediction, a device for "discovering" what a price will be as time unfolds. If more people wished to buy than to sell at a given price, the index futures contract would ratchet up; if more people wanted to sell, it would ratchet down. At 5 percent margin, if the index was at 300, the purchaser (and seller) would have to put up earnest money of $7,500. The price of the contract moved in increments of 5¢—that is, the up-tick from 300 was 300.05, and the down-tick was 299.95. Times 500: $25 per tick. Unlike the situation in the stock market, where the number of shares for each corporation is fixed and buyers must find sellers, futures contracts could be created whenever someone wanted to buy and someone else was willing to sell. Potentially, the number of contracts was unlimited, with no concern about corners because there was no right to delivery. On the contract's last day the entire "open interest" would be extinguished by cash payments and cash receipts.

Maintenance margin on a contract was likely to be 3 percent, or $4,500 for an S&P index contract acquired at 300. If the price went under 294 (or over 306), the buyer (or seller) would have to put up more money or see his contract sold out before the changing price created a loss to his clearing broker, who, by the rules of the exchange, was liable for losses in a customer account that the customer couldn't cover. If the price went up, the buyer could take cash out of his account and the seller would be hit with a margin call; if it went down, the seller could take cash and the buyer would have to deposit more margin. On the day the contract expired, it was worth the index number times 500; if the buyer (seller) had bought (sold) when the contract was worth less (more) than that number, he had a profit; if the seller (buyer) had sold (bought) when it was worth less (more) than that number, he had a loss. All the contracts that survived the trading to the end were settled in this manner, by payments to or from the clearing corporation, and everyone turned his attention to the next contract. Contracts ran three months from inception to expiration (anyone could buy in or sell at any time almost until the end of the three months, creating new contracts with a duration from that day to the preset date of expiration), and there was a new one every quarter.

What must be remembered is that trading this contract when it was new, in 1982–1983, *was* a game. The commodities contracts all came into existence because the makers and users of the commodity needed futures markets—as, indeed, the Soviet and East European economies need them now. The financial futures contracts prior to the S&P contract were also crafted to serve commercial purposes. They were instruments that contributed to the value added by the financial sector of the economy. T-bonds and currencies *were* commodities—one U.S. Treasury bond or yen was like another— and they could be traded as commodities. The S&P contract was derivative not from the stock market but from the betting rings at Ladbroke's. It would be the ultimate tool for the speculators who worked the pits of the agricultural commodities markets. Though Melamed may well have had a vision of something grander, the contract when new was a device for gambling. It was not capitalism, not even casino capitalism (as Keynes called the stock exchanges); it was straight plain vanilla casino. One stock was *not* like another, and the stocks were *not* commodities.

The question of whether the traded index contract was any different from a bet at Ladbroke's remained open in England until 1991. The Gaming Acts of 1845 and 1892 made gambling debts unenforceable in court. Following the 1986 Financial Services Act (England's "Big Bang"), a company called City Index gave a twenty-one-year-old customer named Spencer Leslie a credit line of £500 (about $850) a week to play the Dow. "City Index's principal business," wrote barrister Rachel Davies, reporting on the case, "was index betting. The essential feature was that the client or punter could win or lose variable amounts depending on the change or anticipated change in indices." Leslie, having guessed wrong on the direction of the Dow, wound up owing City Index about $80,000. He asserted that he could not be sued for it, because it was a gambling debt. His counsel argued that "The suggestion that if you dressed up a bet as a hedging operation it was all right, but if you frankly called it a bet it was unacceptable, was very unattractive."

City Index argued in response that paragraph 9 of Part 1 of Schedule 1 of the Financial Services Act had included in the category of investments "Rights under a contract for differences or under any other contract the purpose *or pretended purpose* of which is to secure a profit or avoid a loss by reference to fluctuations in . . . an index" [italics added]. The court agreed with the bookmaker, though somewhat uncomfortably: "The law did not normally take kindly to pretences, yet here was a statute legitimizing a contract which might involve a pretence."[4] Thus in Britain, as in the United States, the purchase of a stock index futures contract with a cash settlement is no longer gambling—legally. And, indeed, it isn't now, for the institutions that are the most frequent purchasers. But it was at the beginning.

Now that Leo Melamed has officially retired from leadership functions at the Merc (with an immense testimonial dinner in early 1991 that pulled together everybody who was anybody in the world of Chicago money), one can perhaps note how important it was to the securities markets that the most influential figure in the development of financial futures was a dedicated gambler. During the trading day, Melamed was never really comfortable unless he had a screen to look at. Chairing meetings of the National Futures Association, the government-authorized self-regulatory body of the futures industry, Melamed would have a telephone brought to the table so he could maintain an open line to his clerk on the floor of the Mercantile Exchange. Conversations with him were interrupted by comments like "That's pretty good; I saw that coming" or "I'm getting *killed* here" as the screen took over his attention, leaving suspended his answers to any questions he had been asked. He is a man of strong feelings, especially for the quixotic cause of keeping the Yiddish language alive. Each year he organizes a Yiddish tribute to the victims of the holocaust. But the only real passion I saw in him in a number of conversations over a period of several years came when he misinterpreted some comment I had made about some comment *he* had made about the course of that day's market. "Martin," he said, "never—I beg you, remember this—never confuse an intraday movement with a trend." And I promised I never would.

The fact that Melamed is a gambler also, I think, refutes the charges that anyone who writes about the Merc hears, usually in the form of unsigned letters on plain paper, from people at the exchange who hate Leo's guts. It is simply impossible to do collusive trading the way Melamed trades, a solitary figure behind a desk designed to hold a semicircle of screens. Nobody watching his exultation at his wins and his worried irritation at his losses could possibly believe that he knew the outcome of his trades before he made them. On the other hand, it must also be said that some of the people he chose to be the nobles around his throne were something less than ornaments of the financial community.

Arbitraging the Index

Given the origins of the S&P contract, it was deliciously suitable that the man who brought it into the mainstream of stock trading was an MIT mathematics teacher who first achieved fame as the world's foremost card reader at the blackjack tables of the great casinos. Because he was able to keep in mind all the cards that had already come out of the four decks in the shoe, Ed Thorp had the odds in his favor as he increased his bets. After a time, all the casinos were alert to his image—a nervous enthusiast, a slim man with very high cheekbones and slightly sunken eyes—and barred him if they saw him in time. Thorp had gravitated to the stock market, where his sort of mind can find lucrative employment tracking the numerology of technical analysis of price movements. It was Thorp who worked out the proportions of 80 or so of the 500 stocks that gave a reasonably good proxy for the index.

The S&P index contract at the Merc traded independently of the stocks, which bothered no one. Setting up the currency futures, Melamed wanted to be certain that the futures prices and the prices in bank forward contracts meshed closely, since the contract was designed to serve the users of foreign currencies. Because the S&P contract was entirely a gaming instrument, its consonance with the prices of the underlying stocks was not important. The consonance would come automatically when the contract was paid off with a cash settlement reflecting its value as calculated from the stock prices rather than as transacted in the commodity pit. It was considered an advantage of the S&P contract that the complexities of trading 500 stocks against the contract would make it impossible to conduct intermarket manipulation.

Inevitably occasions arose when the price of the index contract was well above or well below the aggregated prices of the stocks in the index. At those moments, a man who knew what to buy and sell and could move fast could make money on a sure thing, selling the index and buying the stocks when the market price of the index was higher than the price of the stocks, or buying the index and selling the stocks when the price of the index was lower than that of the stocks. As Thorp moved into this sort of trading for his firm (Princeton-Newport Partners, which later got into terrible trouble, though Thorp himself was never involved, for its supporting role in the Mike Milken tragicomedy), the New York Stock Exchange quite inadvertently eased his labors by adopting electronic order systems that would permit the preprogramming of a computer to buy or sell the shares of several hundred companies at once, through the specialists' posts. (The result is not *quite* instantaneous: A working paper commissioned by the exchange in 1990 estimated a delay of "several seconds" before the order reached the NYSE Common Message Switch, which can handle 210 messages per second; five seconds from the CMS to the specialist's post; and "an average of about 25 more seconds . . . for the specialist to execute the order. . . . In June 1989, 90 seconds would typically elapse between NYSE receipt of the first and last order in a large program trade.")[5]

Conceived as an aid to the small investor, this Designated Order Turnaround (DOT) system knocked most of the cost and risk out of what came to be called "index arbitrage." By 1986, when the market began to heave and split in the preliminaries to the October 1987 earthquake, several dozen investment houses and advisers were running trading programs—some involving as many as 400 of the 500 S&P stocks—to permit profits to be taken from any difference between the index contract as sold at the Merc and the index value as calculated from the prices of the underlying stocks.

By now the appetite for index contracts had been much enlarged by the analyses of the finance economists. The stocks in the contract at 300 cost $150,000. Let us assume an institution with $15 million to invest. It can buy $15 million worth of the stocks in the index, or one hundred index contracts. If it buys the 500 stocks, the brokerage costs will be about $60,000. With the return on the S&P at 3.5 percent, the dividend income on these stocks for three months will be $131,250. Net income for three months will be about $70,000, plus or minus the gains or losses from rising or falling stock prices.

An institution can instead buy one hundred index contracts with a total worth of $15 million. The margin that will have to be deposited with the clearing corporation on such a purchase by an institution is 3 percent, or $450,000. (Institutions are held to lower margin requirements.) These deposits remain the customers' money, and come back to them if the index closes at their purchase price. They will probably have to forgo the interest on the money, which at an 8 percent rate to institutional borrowers would be about $9,000 for three months. The commission to a futures broker for buying one hundred index contracts would probably be $5,000. The cost of buying one hundred index futures contracts, therefore, and holding them for three months, is about $14,000. The institution retains $14,545,000 that it can put into Treasury bills. Assume a T-bill yield of 7 percent. Income to the institution from T-bills for three months is roughly $255,000. Total return for the institution for three months is $241,000 in income plus or minus whatever happens to the price of the 500 stocks in the index contract. And the value of the change in the stock prices is the same, whether the institution buys the index or the stocks.

At the end of the period, of course, the institution that bought the stocks still owns them and will keep all the dividend income without paying any brokerage commission. Instead of being $190,000 better off at the end of the quarter than the institution that bought the stocks, the institution that bought the index will be only $110,000 better off.

It isn't, in fact, quite that simple. Because the market understands the advantages to the institution in holding index contracts rather than real stocks, the index will normally sell at a premium over the underlying stocks by somewhere from $\frac{1}{2}$ to 1 percent, depending on how long the contract has to run. On expiration day, the price of the contract and the price of the stocks converge to determine the cash settlement.

The value of holding the index rather than the stocks is a function of the T-bill rate at any moment of time. The higher the interest rate, the better the odds that an institution will hold the index rather than the stocks—and the greater the premium at which the index contract will sell by comparison with the 500 underlying stocks. Rising interest rates will cause money to wash into the index markets, some of it out of the stock markets. Falling interest rates will cause money to wash out of the index markets, some of it into the stock markets. The Federal Reserve, in acting to change short-term interest rates suddenly, principally affects not economic activity or even inflation but the prices of financial instruments. Henry Kaufman in 1986 unhappily argued ("I wish it were not so") that because "Substantial interest-rate volatility is here to stay . . . bonds are bought more for their price appreciation potential than for their income protection."[6] Interest rate changes in an era of domination by the index futures contract will have as great an impact on stock prices as they do on bond prices.

Bond prices drop when interest rates rise, and rise when interest rates drop, because different interest rate environments change the discount applied to the cash flow from their known interest payments to determine their value. New bonds must offer coupons at current rates or they cannot be sold, and old bonds cannot be priced on a basis different from that of new bonds. Stocks, too, are measured by the discounted value of future cash payments. Here, however, the question has always been the anticipated size of the earnings expected from this stock in future years. Because equity investments traditionally have been made for a long term, the assumption in pricing them has been that interest rates will average out to the 3 percent over the inflation rate that Sidney Homer hypothesized half a century ago in his famous studies for Salomon Brothers. And the inflation rate was considered at worst neutral for stocks. Bonds have only nominal value, because they repay what they borrowed and no more. But equity shares have real value: The assets they represent should rise in price at whatever rate the currency depreciates. Historically, indeed, stocks have been regarded as a hedge against inflation.

No more. Now when interest rates rise the stock market falls just about pari passu with the bond market, and when interest rates fall *or are expected to fall,* the rising tide floats all the boats. Stocks clearly not much influenced by interest rate changes (food companies and broadcasters, for example), move about as much as those obviously dominated by interest rates (housing, utilities). Indeed, it can be even worse than that. As I pointed out in *Barron's* shortly after the event, the Iraqi invasion of Kuwait, by deep-sixing the S&P index contract, produced an instant drop in the shares of the oil service industry stocks that were part of the index, though obviously those companies would be getting a lot of extra business whatever happened in the Gulf. Sanford Grossman of the Wharton School has tried gallantly to defend such nonsense, arguing that "A stock does not have an intrinsic value determined by knowledge of its own payoffs. It has a value as a component in a larger portfolio. . . . Therefore, when the market goes down this tends to lower the value of any single stock even if its own payout stream is expected to be unchanged."[7] When stocks seem reluctant to march in lockstep, the financial economists blame the stocks. The markets in which stocks are traded, write Lawrence Harris, George Sofianos, and James E. Shapiro, "discover index values less efficiently than does the futures market."[8]

As interest rates rise, institutional investors not only put more of their portfolios into higher-yielding bonds but also put more of their equities investment money into index futures and less into the stocks themselves. The purchase of an index contract (which can be created at any time by anybody in the trading pit or at a screen) does not affect prices as much as the purchase of the stocks (which are at any time in fixed supply). Because the buying power of the institutions has moved away from the real market to the derivatives market, stock prices tend to fall.

When interest rates drop, institutional investors find both the bond market and the index contract less rewarding. They buy the equities rather than debt instruments, and the underlying stocks rather than the index, moving all the stocks higher. In both cases, this shift of money between stock and derivative markets heightens the impact of the asset allocation changes also dictated by movements of interest rates. At many pension funds, for example, managers are instructed to move money from lower- to higher-yielding forms of investment when the interest rate available on bonds is three times the dividends available on stocks. Conversely, as interest rates come down, the managers are supposed to take their profits on the bonds and move the money into stocks.

As time goes on, the role of the index future seems likely to enlarge. T-bill rates would have to fall well below 5 percent, which means that inflation would have to be close to zero before the income advantage of index investing washes out completely. Even then, the purchaser of the index would retain the cost advantage of lower brokerage and of a market where prices move in ticks of 5¢ rather than ticks of 12½¢, and where, according to James F. Gammill, Jr., and André F. Perold of the Harvard Business School, spreads between bid and asked average one-tenth what they are on the floor of the stock exchange.

"The demands of 'macro' investors who buy and sell diversified portfolios," Gammill and Perold write, "have permanently changed the way markets work. In particular, the success of stock index futures—which are good surrogates for diversified portfolios—is no fluke, but rather attributable to the inherent cost advantage they offer over trading in individual stocks. Over the long term, stock index markets will attract an increasing share of trading volume, as investors continue to adopt macro trading strategies and to implement them by trading indexes instead of individual stocks."

Gammill and Perold point out some of the implications of this growing move toward index investments. Index investors are "informationless" with regard to individual stocks. Dealing with informationless investors, market-makers can afford to operate on very low markups. As more large investors move to this sort of trading, a higher proportion of the trading in individual stocks is done by what Gammill and Perold call "information traders." Their odds of beating the market-makers are considerably better than those of other people, because they know something other people don't know. To protect themselves against traders who have "stock-specific information," market-makers in the individual stocks have to widen the spread between their bid and their asked. Spreads on Xerox and Eastman Kodak stock have long been a little wider than spreads on other major corporate stocks, because a lot of the trading is done by the trust department of Lincoln First Bank in Rochester, New York, where both companies are headquartered. Market-makers know Lincoln First knows more than they do about the value of these companies.

"[T]here will," Gammill and Perold write, "be something of a spiraling effect that will put further pressure on spreads. Those macro investors who have not yet migrated now have an even greater incentive to do so, while the micro investors [who buy individual stocks] must reconsider their trading strategies in light of the higher transaction costs. . . . [M]ore micro investors . . . will find it more attractive to change their stripes and become macro investors. . . . At the very least, we envision macro markets gaining in liquidity at the expense of deteriorating liquidity in the micro market."[9]

John J. Morton, an earnest Bostonian who ran securities trading for Dewey Square Investors, saw such a future as early as July 1985, when he published an article in *The Pickard Washington Report,* a monthly newsletter from a lawyer once a senior bureaucrat at the SEC. "Brokers at every level," Morton wrote, "have rushed in to take advantage of this arbitrage, mainly in their own proprietary accounts. The past year has witnessed more growth from this form of trading than from customer or agency trading. If this product continues to deliver substantial excess returns, it has the potential to divert enormous sums to the equity market and in the process shift the focus of the equity market from individual issues to groups or baskets of issues."

Laszlo Birinyi, Jr., formerly director of equities research for Salomon and now proprietor of his own technical research service, half seriously sees a time coming when the institutions won't own stock at all. Now there are various indexes for the U.S. stock market as a whole, and for all the major foreign markets. One can buy or sell the indexes; one can buy or sell options on the indexes (the S&P option—actually, on the top 100 rather than the top 500 stocks—is the most heavily traded at the Chicago Board Options Exchange). Wall Street houses have also packaged put and call "warrants" on Tokyo's Nikkei index (issued in the name of highly reputable entities like the Kingdom of Denmark, which takes a cut); for a while in summer 1990, when the Tokyo stock market was in free fall, these warrants were the most heavily traded pieces of paper on the American Stock Exchange, where they were listed. Hideashi Yamashita of the Tokyo Stock Exchange, speaking at a New York Stock Exchange–sponsored meeting in San Francisco, noted that in Japan "the cash market discovers the price of the index. There is a danger that these derivative markets abroad could convey panic to the home market. People developing such derivatives," he added, not without an element of menace, "should respect the integrity of the cash market."

Birinyi expects that there will soon be warrants for indexes expressing the price of stocks in the leading companies in an industry. The investment houses love these instruments, which offer underwriting profits plus the chance to make a good deal of money buying and hedging the warrants.[10] "Why buy Japanese stocks," Birinyi asks, "when you can buy Kingdom of Denmark warrants? Why should CALPERS [California Public Employees Retirement System, the nation's largest investor] buy shares in Lilly if it can buy Bankers Trust drug warrants? What happens to a corporation when it has no stockholders?" Or, as Jack Morton put it, "The tail is not wagging the dog. The dog has moved to Chicago." It isn't even all bad from the broker's point of view, if he's got a Chicago office, too. "The beauty of derivatives," said NYSE specialist Don Stone sourly, "is that they self-destruct every month, and you get another commission."

Meanwhile, the improvement of index arbitrage tactics increases the opportunity for investment houses to trade one market against another, to use for their own benefit in one market information about institutional orders to which they are privy in another market, and to create price movements in one market that will open up profitable trades in the other. "The money," says New York Stock Exchange president Richard Grasso with some distaste, "is in making inequities between like instruments." Much of the effort that was once directed to conducting the agency business on Wall Street now goes to creating inequities between like instruments.

CHAPTER 5

Sure Things

Neither stock brokerage nor investment banking is a profession by the normal definitions of that term. There are essentially no examinations for entry (the tests that control licensure as a registered representative can be coached for in a few weeks), no "mystery" in the medieval sense, no commitment to public service, and very few codes of conduct other than those laid down by law or government regulation. Salomon Brothers' attempt to profit by manipulating the process by which the U.S. government sells debt caused trouble for the firm *only* because its actions violated some recently imposed technical rules. The self-regulatory bodies are a convenience for the official regulators rather than independent rule-making bodies. Their rules, indeed, must be approved by the Securities and Exchange Commission before they can be put into effect, a situation that worked significantly against real self-regulation when John Shad and David Ruder were the chairmen of the SEC.

The normal legal rules of agency and fiduciary obligation have always applied to brokerage, however; there is common-law fraud here as well as statutory fraud. There has never been any question but that frontrunning (purchasing for your own account something your customer has asked you to purchase for him) is a dishonest activity. From early on, the National Association of Securities Dealers, under pressure from the SEC, forbade what was called "riskless principal trading," that is, taking an excessive and/or unreported markup rather than a commission on securities acquired to fill an already entered customer order. Because there are only legal rather than professional standards in this business, however, there was no penalty even to reputation from the discovery and exploitation of loopholes in the law. Once "derivative" securities were being traded in liquid markets, and arbitrage between such markets was part of the routine source of income of insiders, the use of market information in one market to create sure profits in another became relatively common.

The first abuse of intermarket frontrunning came in the options market soon after it opened in 1973. The American stock market had offered options contracts for many years, through an over-the-counter market where tailor-made instruments were bought and sold by members of the Put & Call Dealers Association for a price of $137.50 plus some measurement of the time value of the option and the price at which it could be exercised. When the Chicago Board of Trade created the Chicago Board Options Exchange to house an auction market in standardized options on heavily traded stocks, the regulators took only a limited interest in what seemed a relatively harmless casino. Options would be sold, presumably, by institutional investors supplementing their investment income and bought by individuals taking a flier on stock prices. The result would be a minor but not trivial addition to market liquidity.

The SEC assumed supervision of the new market (one of the reasons it had to be a separate institution was that the Chicago Board of Trade wanted nothing to do with the SEC), and imposed some minimal rules on member firms. Each firm had to appoint someone to be its Registered Options Principal, who would pass an examination on options and the trading thereof. The questions asked in the printed instruction program were identical to those asked in the test, and everyone passed. Then the market took off—in 1976, options trading accounted for nearly one-tenth of Merrill Lynch's commission income—and the rules were tightened. In 1980, SEC chairman Harold Williams pushed through an Intermarket Surveillance System which gives the regulators a reasonable crack at matching action in the options pits and on the Stock Exchange floor, though it takes three days to sort the data.

Also in 1980, the exchange put out an "Information Memo" presenting its

> views with respect to certain practices generally referred to as "front-running of blocks." Because a block transaction in an underlying security may have an impact on the market for that security or the options covering that security (or vice versa), the Exchange cautions its members that they should not trade in options or in underlying securities by taking advantage of their possession of material non-public information concerning block transactions in these securities. The Exchange wishes to emphasize that this kind of activity on the part of market professionals may give rise to a proceeding under Exchange Rule 476 alleging conduct inconsistent with just and equitable principles of trade.[1]

Before the new rules, however, the brokerage houses found some glittering sure things in the interstices of the interface between options and the underlying stocks. The options market (like the futures markets) operates on a basis of hand signals communicated from clerks at telephones. In Chicago, these clerks sit at desks on stepped-up rows along the wall. Formerly, when a member firm in New York got a large order from an institutional customer, the representative processing the order (or his clerk, for his own account) passed the word to the order clerk in Chicago, who would wigwag the information to his trader on the floor, who would buy an option on the securities involved. If the word from New York was a purchase order, the trader bought a call (giving him the right to buy what would be a rising stock at a price fixed before the rise); if it was a sell order, he bought a put (giving him the right to sell what would be a falling stock at a price fixed before the fall).

Within a matter of minutes, the impact of the purchase or sale in the "cash" market in New York would be felt in the options pit, and the transaction could then be reversed, or the option exercised at the close of day. This was shooting fish in a barrel, and rather diminished the number of independent traders who were willing to risk their own money in the options pits. In part at the urging of the CBOE itself, the SEC stepped in and wrote regulations forbidding frontrunning between the two trading floors. Oddly enough, directly manipulative "self-frontrunning" activity was not prohibited, and the New York firm of Miller, Tabak & Hirsch publicly bought heavily on the New York Stock Exchange on April 19, 1984, when the options contracts were expiring, to push some "out-of-the-money" call options (options to buy at a price above current market) "into the money" (giving them value as the price of the stocks rose above the option price as both markets closed for the day). In 1985, in Information Memo 85–36 the exchange extended its prohibition of frontrunning to index options, still without reference to self-frontrunning.

Regarding the S&P index contract traded at the Chicago Mercantile Exchange, however, matters were murkier. Orders to buy or sell individual stocks would not move the S&P contract price. Even orders to buy or sell all the stocks in the index, by an index investor, would not necessarily move the contract. No doubt, it could happen: Indeed, there is considerable evidence that it *did* happen on December 19, 1986, a "triple-witching day" on which option contracts, futures contracts, and options on futures expired. On that day, Salomon Brothers purchased index futures contracts for its own account in Chicago shortly before placing a one *billion* dollar order for stocks in the S&P basket, transforming a market that was down about ten Dow points to a market that closed up more than sixteen points.

Only very large orders in New York could produce such movements, however. Enough stocks to make a hundred contracts would cost some millions of dollars ($5 million in the early 1980s, $15 million in the late 1980s), and a hundred contracts were almost certainly not enough to move the Chicago price. The Merc on a normal day traded fifty thousand or more S&P 500 contracts. But the tail might wag the dog—five hundred contracts, which almost certainly would move the price (sometimes by quite a lot, as locals in the pits added their demand to the trend), could be bought in Chicago on margin of only two and a half a million dollars. At the Stock Exchange, traders have to pay (in five days) only on their net position at the close of trading. Someone who knew what an institution that bought indexes was about to do in Chicago could make a killing in New York, with a very small investment.

As there was so much index arbitrage by market insiders, "riskless principal trading" between the markets did not stand out. Because the two markets were regulated by different government agencies—Chicago by the Commodity Futures Trading Commission (CFTC)—there was no single authority that could investigate intermarket trading and police it. Both the Merc and the New York Stock Exchange insisted that there was no problem that couldn't be handled in the normal course of business. Participants knew better: As PaineWebber put it in a 1988 memo, "The buy side trader . . . sees the volume and he sees what is happening in the intermarket trading between futures and stocks, and he feels its impact." In April 1988, six months after the great crash that had been exacerbated by intermarket trading, the staff of the New York Stock Exchange proposed a rule that would at least limit the use of information on customer intentions in one market to give brokers a sure-thing bet for their own accounts in the other.

The proposed rule is worth quoting in its entirety:

> When a member or person associated with a member or member organization is in possession of material non-public market information concerning one or more baskets of stock, the execution of which affects the value of an index, trading in futures on that index before information concerning the execution of the stock basket(s) has been made publicly available, to take advantage of the non-public information, may violate just and equitable principles of trade.

The rule was interesting in what it left out. There was no prohibition here: The exchange was merely proposing that such intermarket trading "may" violate just and equitable principles. The rule would not touch the most common source of such cheating, the leakage of information to other participants in the market in return for allocated commissions, "soft dollars," or reciprocal leaks. Most important of all, the rule spoke only to trading futures on the index before the execution of customer orders at the exchange. It did not speak to the practice of trading on the exchange with knowledge of what customers were about to do in the futures market.

Many traders felt that such activity was commonplace, and disgraceful. "What greater inside information could you ever have as a firm," Richard Heckman of Prudential-Bache rhetorically asked members of the House Subcommittee on Telecommunications and Finance in a hearing in May 1988, "than to know there was a $700 million asset allocation program coming that day? . . . You would do those trades for no commission if you had that information. . . . Large institutions with computer access to the floors of the futures exchanges and the New York Stock Exchange, have every ability to manipulate stock prices and futures prices and can frontrun their own program trades."[2]

Robert A. Kanter is a professional arbitrageur and former specialist at the American Stock Exchange, a small, energetic man with a black pompadour who wears a jacket to work at a screen at his five-man trading desk in the office building beside Trinity Church. He gave the Senate Banking Committee the populist perspective:

> Individual investors and other market participants are continuously entering into transactions with parties who possess material non-public market information, the result being a transfer of untold sums of dollars from one group to another. Eventually, if not stopped, public confidence in our markets will erode and the individual investor will be forced out of the market. In addition, professional traders and on-floor market-makers, who have been taking "the other side" of the front-runners' trades, eventually will be unable to compete and will exit the market. Unless a series of corrective measures are implemented, . . . this abusive trading practice will ultimately destroy the liquidity, depth and integrity of our markets.

Nevertheless, the proposal met angry opposition at several of the largest brokerage houses. Counsel for one of them said in privileged conversation, "I don't like that proposed rule. According to one reading, you could say that we are in violation when we agree to sell a basket of stocks to a customer at the closing prices plus ten cents a share, and protect ourselves during the day by purchasing some index futures in Chicago. We do that all the time."

In Chicago, the proposed rule was looked upon as an example of chauvinism by the stock exchange, as an effort to contain the growing power of the Chicago markets. Less than 20 percent of the trading in New York was computer-controlled "program" trading that would have obvious index implications, but well over three-quarters of the trading in Chicago related one way or another to purchases and sales in New York. In addition, the SEC, absorbed as it then was with the fear that the stock market would become less liquid in the aftermath of the crash, opposed the adoption of the NYSE rule on the grounds that it might remove some players from the market. The Division of Market Regulation suggested to the Stock Exchange that a rule be worked out jointly with the Merc to control whatever abuses the two exchanges agreed had to be eliminated. Given the resistance of its own largest members, the NYSE withdrew the rule and began what would be a year-long negotiation with the Merc. What emerged was a rule agreed on by the boards of both exchanges, and accepted by both the SEC and the CFTC on July 19, 1989.

The ensemble of "NYSE Frontrunning Interpretations" was issued by the exchange on November 27, 1989. The wording was chewier and weighed down with legalese, but the line of approach was not much different from what it had been.[3] The verb form "may be" still dominated the sentence. There was a list of those covered by the rules: "These restrictions apply to trading and the handling of orders by floor members, upstairs traders and all employees of members and member organizations. For example, floor brokers and upstairs traders who have knowledge of an order that will be executed imminently may not give this information to any other person, nor the terms of the order, for the purpose of having that person take advantage of the information."

The five descriptions of situations where trading for one's own account might make a problem were similar to the description in the proposal of eighteen months before, with one very important exception: the word "imminent" had been added to each one. In the intermarket context, the criticism now applies only to "a transaction in any stock index futures contract or option on a stock index future when such member or person has acquired knowledge of the *imminent* execution of another person's stock program transaction."

Moreover, the practice of trading against the customer, of acting as a riskless principal, is given qualified approval: "Nothing herein shall prevent such member or person from establishing, in a futures market, a bona fide hedge of risk such member or person may have assumed or agreed to assume in facilitating the execution of any other person's stock program orders or stock index options orders." There remains some discomfort: "The risk to be hedged must be the result of having established a position or having given a firm commitment to assume a position, and the offsetting hedging transaction must be commensurate with such risk." The exchange protects, however, the practice of buying the index in Chicago while in possession of an order to buy the stocks at the close. This gives the house a stake in having the prices move on the exchange in a direction adverse to the interests of its customer, and an all but guaranteed profit if the customer's order is large enough to move the market.

Also protected by the final rule, though somewhat reluctantly, was a practice the trade now wished to have known as "legging" rather than "self-frontrunning."[4] The difference between conventional frontrunning and self-frontrunning was described by Morgan Stanley in a submission to the SEC as something beyond the understanding of mere bureaucrats: "Issues concerning 'self-frontrunning' are considerably more complex and involve considerations of fairness and harm about which many disagree." In fact, the only difference is the origin of the order that moves the price. The key fact is that brokerage houses playing for their own account ("proprietary strategies") are able to assure profits for themselves by exploiting intermarket opportunities.

Self-frontrunning turns out to be the functional equivalent of the 1920s "pool" operation. I am indebted to Gerald Beirne of Thomson McKinnon Securities for the explanation of how it works, which is as follows:

The "proprietary strategy" begins with the acquisition of a large number of S&P 500 contracts, on insider margin of 1 percent. Not much cash is required, because as the price runs up the purchaser can finance his future purchases with the quickly

credited profits on his earlier purchases. Given the nature of the
trading pit's reaction to price movements in futures contracts
("the trend is your friend"), the house can probably expect others
to join in pushing up the price of the contracts.

Once the futures contract "leg" is in place, the house begins
purchasing the stocks itself. This does take a large capital
investment, reduced once again by the likelihood that other
bidders will come into the market to help. As this stage of the
strategy ends, the house has large positions in the underlying
stocks as well as its large positions in the index futures, and the
market is rising smartly. "But it must be emphasized," Beirne
noted in his letter to the SEC criticizing the Stock Exchange's
proposed rule, "that these positions were acquired *solely* for their
role in guaranteeing the profits that result from a successfully
executed self-frontrunning program. They serve no legitimate
purpose whatsoever."

Even before completing its stock-purchasing program, the self-
frontrunning house begins selling the futures contracts previously
acquired, at a very large profit, the price having been driven up
twice, first by the house's own activities in the futures pits and
then by its activities in the underlying market. And it does not
merely dispose of these contracts—it keeps selling (in effect going
short the futures contracts, an entirely legal activity whether the
market is rising or falling) until it has a considerable stake in the
further decline of a market which has already begun to fall in
response to its futures selling.

At this point, the house begins to dump the stocks acquired
during the second phase of its self-frontrunning strategy, not
caring how low the market goes because any losses suffered on
these sales are automatically repaid by the gains on the recently
sold futures contracts. Again, others pile on to catch the trend,
increasing the profits the house makes on its short position in the
futures pits.

Except that the pool operators of the 1920s did not have the
cover of the intermarket transaction to conceal their activities
(which were indeed trumpeted as the last word in sophistication:
A family fortune that paid for a presidency, two U.S. senatorships
and at least one congressional seat rested on just such tactics by
the late Joseph P. Kennedy), self-frontrunning is conceptually

identical to what used to be considered the worst abuse of the market in the years before government regulation and stock exchange surveillance. Communication being much quicker today, a full self-frontrunning exercise can be pulled off in a single day's trading, whereas the pools normally required several days or even weeks to mature. Intraday volatility is now greater than it was seventy years ago, but interday volatility (which is what the finance professors measure) is reduced. The exchange worries about this maneuvering—its frontrunning memo notes that someone "execut[ing] a transaction in one market to take advantage of [his own] imminent transaction in a related market . . . may be engaging in manipulative activity." But the rules continue to permit it.

Beirne makes the interesting point that a high proportion of what appear to be "index arbitrage" transactions by brokers for their own account are probably related to pool operations of this sort. The theory of index arbitrage holds that participants in the markets who are fast on their feet can take advantage of discrepancies that open up between the price of the futures contract and the prices of the underlying stocks. But even in the day of SuperDot and virtually automatic order execution for 2100 shares or less, it is not easy to buy all the stocks in a relevant basket at the price for which they were selling at the instant when the apparent gap opened between the index futures price and the calculated price in the cash market. That price, after all, is the most recent sale. The current offered price, which is what the buyer will probably have to pay if he ships a market order to the post electronically, will be at least one-eighth of a point higher than the last sale price. ("Probably," because a specialist can, and sometimes does, "stop" an order at the price of the last sale, promising to execute it at that price if the market moves as the customer expects, but at a better price if a better price becomes available. The order shows as "stopped" at one side of his screen.)

About 3500 shares must be bought to match the index. That eighth of a point means $450, or almost a full point on the index contract, in the market impact cost of execution (we are assuming proprietary transactions, which do not incur out-of-pocket commission costs—indeed, in the days of SuperDot, they do not even incur significant opportunity costs). If any number of participants are trying to buy (or sell) at the same time, the gap between the calculated price of the stocks in the index and the price the arbitrageur will have to pay will jump something more than an eighth. One hundred contracts implies about 12,000 shares of IBM; get half a dozen characters trying that game at the same time, and even the most liquid stock on the floor is going to jolt up or down with some violence.

Thus, as Ed Thorp noted sadly in 1987, the money went out of straight observational sure-thing index arbitrage as more players entered the game. By 1991, there were only five firms repeatedly engaged in such activity with heavy volume: Kidder Peabody, Morgan Stanley, Bear Stearns, Susquehanna Associates, and Salomon. It is all but impossible to believe that they were in fact earning their returns from this activity by passively reacting to differences in the movements of the futures contract and the calculated index, especially in light of the fact that Kidder and Morgan were the most vigorous opponents of any effort to extend the intermarket rules to self-frontrunning.

The precipitousness and size of the market moves attributed to "index arbitrage" can be explained by a theory that speculators pile on to ride a trend, but the stronger argument is that the movements are planned and manipulative. "The truth today," James Coxon, chairman of the investment policy committee at CIGNA, a giant insurance company, told a House committee in summer 1990, "is that stock-index futures are used by a small group that had determined how to game the system and benefit from volatility that is excessive, unnecessary, and perhaps induced."

No less a figure than I. W. "Tubby" Burnham, former chairman of Drexel Burnham and of the Securities Industry Association, wrote in a letter to *The Wall Street Journal* that "Those who really handle the large amounts of institutional money have the discretion to buy and sell whenever they wish and increase the volatility on both sides."[5]

Once upon a time, the SEC took a strong interest in this sort of finagling. "Where floor traders rush to a security in which buying exists or is anticipated," a release from the commission said in 1964, "and, by a succession of purchases at rising prices, interspersed with those of the public, arouse and capitalize upon public reaction to the activity shown on the tape, the consequences are hardly distinguishable from those of a manipulation, whether or not a violation of Section 9 of the Exchange Act is intended or can be established."[6] At least since the first deregulatory fervor struck the Carter administration, however, the SEC has not felt such matters to be of serious concern. The quick eight- to twenty-point moves created by heavy index arbitrage activity are noted daily, and the noters pass on.

These index arbitrage moves are entirely consonant with the market operations the SEC decried in 1964. John A. Mendelson, then senior vice president and head of the market analysis group at Dean Witter, laid out the scenario in one of his periodic papers about his friend "Benny the Trader," who had moved from New York to Chicago because "this is where the action is." Benny's card identified his new corporate name as "Personalized Markets, Inc.," and his advertising slogan was "Markets any way you like them." Benny had been a pioneer of index arbitrage, and had previously explained to his buddy John the mechanics of "the basis," the gap between the price of the futures contract and the calculated price of the basket of real stocks that was necessary to make index arbitrage profitable. Now he had moved on:

> "It occurred to me that, although I was making a fortune, there was still a greater one to be made. The program guys needed leadership. The robots needed a general to grab the ring in their nose and jerk them around. I decided Benny the Trader and a few of his Chicago friends would become the generals. . . .
>
> "You would be surprised at how many clients we have in only six months. We never ask questions about their motives and we never do anything that is in violation of the securities laws. We also charge $150,000 a day for our service. You want the market to open up 10, then turn down 20 points, and close flat? No problem. All we do is move the basis and the $100 billion behind us [the amount of money estimated to be in index funds as of December 1986, when Mendelson wrote this piece] does the rest. . . . All we do is move the basis and the rest is automatic."
>
> "Benny, you are manipulating the market! My friend, the great Benny the Trader, is a crook." "No, no . . . we only move the nearby future, that is all. Why is that illegal? The rest is a reflex action. . . . [I]t takes care of itself. . . . You can call it manipulation, but we like to say we are providing creative leadership for the

billions and billions in the hands of robots. We say jump and they
jump. We say up 10, back down 15 and then up 20 and the
program guys say your wish is our command. . . . You're a pro, you
must have noticed that every intraday movement either up or down
in the past four weeks has started in Chicago."[7]

Interviewed in 1989, Mendelson was a graceful man in his
forties with long memories of the New York Stock Exchange. His
father had worked as a specialist on the floor for forty-eight years.
"He used to tell me about 'trolling,' setting the bait for public
customers, and about all the painting the tape [sales brokers
colluded to advertise fake transactions at prearranged prices]. In
the twenties the senior partners of the brokerage houses worked
on the floor, because there was so much bullshit going on you
wanted a senior man." He did not claim to have proof of
frontrunning. "You have to be physically on the trading desk to
prove it," he said, "but once you see it on the machine, you know
it's there. My eyes tell me that B doesn't happen before A." The
Benny the Trader piece was an observation by an insider, not a
reaction to public discontent with the market; it appeared almost a
year before the October 19, 1987, crash.

One must also note in passing that whereas the Chicago Merc
has signed off on the limited rules governing intermarket trading,
the Chicago Board of Trade has not. The Major Market Index, a
futures contract on twenty large-capitalization stocks (including
seventeen of the thirty in the Dow), trades on the CBOT. General
counsel Scott Early of the CBOT told *Business Week* at the time of
the agreement between the NYSE and the Merc that his exchange
had refused to sign off because the new rules "didn't guard
against the prohibition of legitimate hedging activity."[8]

One tactic that remains unpoliced and fairly common is a triple
play using all three markets. A trader buys calls on the options
exchange and then aggressively buys stocks in New York,
meanwhile selling a futures contract in Chicago to hedge the risk
of loss on the newly acquired stocks. The profits made on the
rising stocks are devoured by the losses on the declining futures,
but the call options rise dramatically in value, and can be cashed in
before reversing the other transactions. The beauty of this operation is that once the purchases and the hedges are in place, the

trader does not care whether the stocks and futures go up or down: His profits are safely in his pocket. This "portfolio strategy" does not work so well when stocks are declining, for reasons we shall look at in the next section.

Manipulation and the Blind Eye

One of the first sure things developed by the investment houses in response to the market in traded options was a combination of a short sale in New York and the purchase of a call option on the Chicago Board Options Exchange. For an outside customer, this would be a relatively expensive proposition, because he would have to pay commissions (very high as a percentage of price in the options market) plus a fee to borrow the stock he sold, and would be required by the rules to leave the proceeds of the sale with his broker, plus 50 percent margin. The broker himself, however, could borrow without charge from his margin customers (part of the margin agreement is permission for the broker to borrow the stock), and could invest all the money received from the sale in Treasury bills, to earn interest. The interest earned on this money would more than cover the price of the call option, and for many of the most widely traded stocks it would also cover the cost of the dividend that the short seller must provide to the owner of the stock he borrowed. If the stock went down, the stock would be bought, profits would be taken on the short sale, and the call option would be thrown in the wastebasket. If the stock went up, the stock would be acquired by exercising the call option, and delivered to the counterparty on the short sale. It was a free ride for member firms.

In theory, such activities could not be carried on when the market was falling, because the New York Stock Exchange in the late 1930s (at the insistence of the future Supreme Court Justice William O. Douglas, who was then chairman of the SEC) had instituted an "up-tick rule," forbidding short sales unless the most recent sale of this stock at a different price had been at a lower price (price of $40½, then 40¼, then 40¼, stock cannot be sold short for 40¼; price of $40¼, 40½, 40½, stock *can* be sold short at 40½). The rule was designed to frustrate what had been the most unpopular and in fact damaging of insider stock trading strategies: the bear raid. In a classic 1920s bear raid, a pool of brokers and the specialist in the stock would begin selling it, meanwhile spreading rumors of trouble in the company.

Psychologically, there is an imbalance between the attitudes of buyers and the attitudes of sellers. Nobody ever *has* to buy, but people have many compelling reasons to sell stocks, everything from a divorce to tuition bills to the purchase of a house or a trip abroad. Panic buying is a term of art—it happens, but mostly to short sellers, who see real losses multiplying as the price of a stock goes up. For others, annoyance at having missed a buying opportunity is more or less controllable. Buying on the way up is seen as taking a risk. Panic selling, however, can become epidemic, as people see their life's savings going down the spout; selling on the way down is seen as avoiding a risk.

One of the analytical disasters from the creation of derivative securities products is the loss of the commonsense understanding that buying and selling are different activities. The purchase of a call option and the purchase of a put option are identical activities, offering limited risk and, in the eyes of the purchasers and those who sell options, all but unlimited reward. (The sale of either option, of course, is a highly risky activity. In the October 19 crash, people who had sold put options, giving their purchasers the right to sell this stock to them at the prices prevailing before the crash, lost twenty and thirty times as much as they had been paid for the options.)

The purchase and sale of a futures contract are in every way identical activities, producing claims by the clearing house on the seller or buyer that are the mirror image of each other. Despite the report of the Brady Commission on the 1987 crash, which argued that the options, futures, and stock markets are really "one market," neither an option nor a futures contract is closely comparable to the purchase or sale of securities themselves. Activities in one of them can be used to manipulate prices in another, but, to say the least, that does not make the three markets one.

Failing to recognize the difference between a call and actual ownership of securities, the SEC in the dying days of the Nixon administration exempted holders of calls on a security from the up-tick rule on short sales, thereby legitimating the pioneers' sure-thing "portfolio strategy." When the commission began to worry about intermarket manipulation of options prices during the Carter administration, it ruled out not only frontrunning but also the claim that possession of a call option gave a trader exemption from the application of the up-tick rule.

By 1986, academic market theorists were becoming concerned about the asymmetry in markets created by the NYSE up-tick rule. If a trader could sell futures contracts or buy put options, why couldn't he sell stock short? This was wildly wrong-headed: In fact, the development of derivative markets made it all the more imperative to control short-selling, because the difference in leverage factors between the derivative markets and the cash markets make volatility in stock prices so much more valuable to insiders. Put options may triple in price when the price of a stock drops by as little as 5 percent. By purchasing put options and then aggressively selling the stock, a market insider can guarantee himself very large profits even if the stock turns around and rises beyond its previous price before he can buy himself out of the short position. Still, traders convinced Richard Ketchum, director of the SEC Division of Market Regulation, that in our brave new world restrictions on short sales were an anachronism, and reduced the funds broker/dealers were willing to commit to trading. In December 1986, as a first step toward their elimination, on the stated grounds that the up-tick rule "was impeding the efficiency of their index arbitrage," the SEC granted Merrill Lynch a letter ruling to the effect that investment houses—provided that *somewhere* in the shop they did have the stock they were selling short in their trading account—would be permitted to make short sales into a declining market as part of an index arbitrage strategy.[9]

How great an effect this ruling had on the market crash nine months later is a subject for debate. Among the stranger pieces of evidence that there might have been an effect is an inadvertent comment by the Commodity Futures Trading Commission, as part of its argument that futures trading could not have been part of the problem. Index arbitrage could not have played a significant role, CFTC wrote in its first report on what had happened, because "the 'uptick rule' on the NYSE inhibits arbitrage-induced short-selling of stocks in a general market decline."[10] CFTC didn't know that as the rule affected broker/dealers trading for their own account, the SEC had opened a loophole large enough to admit the entry of lots of short sales.

Combining the reports of the CFTC and the SEC,[11] one sees 5700 index futures contracts bought on October 19 by broker/dealers who were members of the New York Stock Exchange, and 11 million shares of stock admittedly sold short on the floor of the NYSE. The $500 million or so in such sales is of course not much by comparison to the $22 billion of total sales that day, but it does amount to about a third of the total capitalization of the specialist firms that were supposed to be maintaining an orderly market and had to provide the buy side for virtually all these sales.

Moreover, purchasing by broker/dealers for their own account, much of it for the purpose of immediate arbitrage profit through sales on the stock exchange floor, provided in some periods as much as half the buy side in the index futures pits, preventing the market in these pits from reflecting the full extent of the panic in the trading community. A number of institutional funds had committed to investment strategies that purported to "insure" the value of stock holdings through "dynamic hedging" in the futures pits. The theory was that losses suffered in a declining stock market would be balanced by profits on the sale of index futures as the price went down. By counterfeiting the presence of demand in the pits, index buying in Chicago for arbitrage purposes by broker/dealer firms may well have encouraged the banks that managed the funds that followed these dynamic hedging policies ("portfolio insurance") to continue their pursuit of this folly, and may have delayed the opening of the gap between the two markets which was in the end the way prices found a floor.

In response to the first publicity given the no-action letter to Merrill Lynch, about two months after the crash, the SEC staff insisted that the intention of the letter had been to deal with only a narrow technical problem, and that the exemption was not meant to apply to index arbitrage in general by the broker/dealer firms. In fact, however, counsel to these firms *had* interpreted it to mean that the purchase of an index contract in Chicago made the firm constructively long the stocks in the index, and thus constituted a blanket exemption from the rule. No-action letters are not the law, though a case in the First Circuit (Boston) once held that such a letter is "drafted in the knowledge that the industry will place heavy reliance on it."[12] (Another case, a few years later, refused credence to an SEC no-action letter because of "the confusion and ambiguity surrounding the SEC interpretation.")[13] In its report on the dark days of October, the SEC Division of Market Regulation said that twelve of the thirteen large broker/dealers that had sold short as part of index arbitrage on October 19 had been "unable to quantify" the extent to which they had relied on the no-action letter.[14]

On January 8, 1988, a report on the still-recent crash was published by a commission headed by former Senator and future Treasury Secretary Nicholas Brady, who had been chairman of Dillon Read. The commission singled out arbitrage-related sales by pension funds totaling about $2 billion, and sales by mutual funds totaling about $900 million, but did not give special attention to proprietary trading. In its conclusion, the report did note that "Speculation by professional market participants is, however, a reasonable concern. . . . [Similar] margins resulting in roughly equivalent risk and leverage between the two market segments are necessary to enforce consistent intermarket public policy objectives concerning leverage and speculation."[15] By an extraordinary coincidence, the Brady Report was launched on a day when the Dow dropped 140 points, the third worst nominal decline in the market's history. This was entirely unexpected: The market had been advancing smartly all week. There was no news story and no apparent fundamental reason for the drop. Stanford law professor Joseph Grundfest, then an SEC commissioner—a "free-market Democrat" who had been entirely sympathetic to synthetic securities and had reacted to the evidence of Salomon's frontrunning with a statement of concern about "opportunistic trading"—commented that "I can explain October 19th; but I can't explain January 8th."

Professionals in both Chicago and New York, traders and managers of funds, found explanation less difficult. They knew—it wasn't just a matter of *belief*—that the dominant force in pushing the market down on January 8 had been proprietary index arbitrage by the big broker/dealers. A few months later, a study of this day's records by the SEC for a committee of the House of

Representatives confirmed the accuracy of their knowledge. In the half-hour period of greatest decline, as much as two-fifths of the trading had been by broker/dealers for their own account.[16] The SEC staff continued to insist, however, that its no-action letter had not played a role in this disaster. Only a small fraction of the selling by broker/dealers on January 8, the staff reported, had been admittedly short, and the SEC did not have access to information about how much of it had been preceded by purchases in Chicago. One could believe if one really tried that nothing had happened but the sort of "unwinding" contemplated in the no-action letter.

In fact, very clearly, the broker/dealers *had* sold short. They can do so without the sort of public audit trail customers must leave, because they have access ad lib to the stocks their margin customers hold in their accounts. One of the most profitable activities of the modern brokerage house is lending out for a fee the stocks in margin accounts; by borrowing the stocks themselves, the proprietary traders give up that income, but they expect to make more. In studying the January 8 decline, the SEC staff admittedly did not investigate whether the broker/dealers had sold short by the definitions that would have applied beyond question before December 1986.

There is some reason to believe that the New York Stock Exchange did inquire, and did not like what it found. In March 1988, the exchange petitioned the SEC for the right to enforce its own up-tick rule against its members, regardless of the no-action letter—and the SEC refused to give consent.[17]

A few weeks later, on April 14, 1988, the roof fell in once more, with another decline of more than a hundred Dow points. Again, Congressman Edward Markey's subcommittee asked for reports from both the CFTC and the SEC, and received diametrically opposed explanations of the role index arbitrage had played in the panic. The CFTC proclaimed that virtually all the sales by broker/dealers were unwindings of previously established short-futures/long-stocks positions. The SEC found that the vast majority of such transactions by broker/dealers involved short sales in the cash market.[18] *All* arbitrage-related short sales in the SEC "Chronology" were proprietary. And the chronology, based on the broker/dealers' own reports, almost certainly understates the fraction of arbitrage-related sales in which the professionals went short. One can hardly believe, for example, that the broker/dealer who thrice sold them at more than $5 million a pop was long all of the more than 1500 different stocks in the basket required to complete an arbitrage against the Value Line index traded in Kansas City.

A footnote in the SEC report accepts a pious assertion by the firms doing this selling that "in any event, it was their practice to execute arbitrage sell orders on plus ticks in down markets and buy order [sic] on minus ticks in rising markets in order to mitigate their effects on market volatility."[19] One is reminded of the story of the gentleman strolling down Piccadilly who mistook the Duke of Wellington for the director of the Royal Academy. "Mr. Arbuthnot, I believe," the gentleman said, bowing. "A man who would believe that," the Duke grumbled in response, "would believe anything." It is of the essence of index arbitrage that the other leg of the transaction be executed immediately, which means that nobody has time to stop and look at ticks. There is virtually no chance that all or even most of the four hundred or so stocks traded in the basket designed to match the index will be sold on up-ticks in a day of rapidly declining prices.

Imposing the Cure

If they so smart, why ain't they rich? If this sort of cheating on the system did indeed become commonplace on Wall Street in the 1980s, why did the industry find itself in 1990 with the lowest profits in its history?

There are several answers. First, a 5¢ per share reduction in average commissions means a loss of about $6 million per day in revenues to brokers handling public orders, which would eat up all the frontrunning profits between the S&P contract and New York if such activity accounted for a quarter of all S&P trading and yielded a full point gain per contract. In the mid-1980s, trading with the natives at the savings and loans (S&Ls) had generated billions of dollars of profit a year (my own informed but inevitably ballpark estimate is an average of $5 billion a year) for the houses that packaged, sold, and traded mortgages and helped the S&Ls

sell their Certificates of Deposit and borrow through "repurchase agreements" to buy more and more such paper. Interest on repurchase agreements alone exceeded $10 billion a year, of which $1.5 billion (again, $6 million a day) was probably profit. In the second half of the decade, fees associated with highly leveraged transactions more than took up the torch that was being dropped from the feeble hands of dying S&Ls.

In addition, the profits from dealing rather than broking listed securities went to a limited number of firms—Morgan Stanley, Salomon, Goldman Sachs, Bear Stearns, plus the boutiques, the floor members and their friends who left the floor and took up residence in the upstairs offices of the specialist firms and clearing brokers. Merrill and Shearson, oriented more toward the larger per-share commissions from individuals, maintained significant trading operations but were more likely to expand in the direction of unpublicized soft-dollar arrangements with the institutions.

There was a degree of danger in getting too prominently identified with intermarket trading. In January 1988, Robert G. Kirby, chairman of the Guardian Capital group of mutual funds and a member of the Brady Commission, let the press know that he had notified all firms heavily engaged in index arbitrage for their own account that he was taking his funds' business elsewhere. Shortly thereafter, with varying degrees of grumbling (Kidder Peabody, which was being held to the very exacting earnings standards of its parent General Electric, was the most reluctant), the houses that did a commission as well as a trading business announced that they would no longer do proprietary index arbitrage. By early 1991, however, all of them except the most heavily consumer-oriented—Merrill, Shearson, Dean Witter, and PaineWebber—were once again doing program trades for their own account.

Except in the minds of the innocent academics and their students in the press, there is simply no question that this is the wrong way to run markets. The Japanese will take care of it in their way, first by a Japanese fix called "slow down," by which traders in futures require five-minute intervals before the price can move again, then by making it impossible for those who use these markets for manipulation to make a profit in Tokyo, something the Ministry of Finance can always arrange. The New York Stock

Exchange, to the resentment of academics and the accompaniment of some grumbling at the SEC, found a way to mitigate the short-term impact of intermarket trading by establishing a fifty-point trigger to activate a more extensive tick rule. All orders to be executed pursuant to an index arbitrage strategy must be marked "IA," and once the Dow has risen or fallen by fifty points, such orders may be executed, stock by stock, *only* if a stock is rising against a falling trend or falling against a rising trend. For the first time, the up-tick rule is symmetrical, matched with a down-tick rule for rising markets, preventing arbitrage from accelerating the movement of stock prices up or down. Another procedure linked to the S&P futures contract directs all electronically entered program trades to a "sidecar" where they must wait five minutes once the S&P contract has declined twelve points (equivalent to one hundred Dow points) in a single day.

As a result, the market survived a downside panic following the Iraqi invasion of Kuwait in August 1990—and an upside panic following the Fed's decision to pump money into the banking system in January 1991—with few days when the Dow moved as much as fifty points, and only one when it moved one hundred points. On November 19, 1991, the fifty-point trigger delayed a 120-point collapse for an hour, but no longer.

Perhaps the clearest demonstration of the effectiveness of the rule was a sudden eruption of newspaper stories to the effect that the imposition of the collar was ineffective, and would drive arbitrage business behind closed doors and overseas because the rule was too much of a burden.[20] NYSE member firms could not carry on such business overseas off the floor during trading hours without violating Rule 390, requiring that orders be exposed at the post. And considering how swiftly the Drexel bankruptcy happened, and the number of customers abroad who got stung, it's hard to imagine a pension fund or charitable endowment that would wish to do rapid-fire programs of secret deals with brokerage houses leveraged fifty to one. In October 1991, the SEC okayed a permanent trigger.

Fundamental distortions are not cured by triggers. The difficulty is not that insiders make money to which they are not entitled and the public loses money it should not lose—unquestionably the result of intermarket trading: Insiders buy stock in the bottom half of the day's price range and sell in the top half, while public customers buy in the top half and sell in the bottom half. The problem, as I wrote in *Barron's,* is a systemic mispricing as the prices of individual stocks come to be determined by the movement of interest rates and tax levies rather than by the success or failure of the companies in which the holders of the stocks own a share. Interest rates are not equally important to all businesses, and changes in the tax code often give advantages to some businesses and disadvantages to others. But the index responds to the average. Like the man who drowned in the lake with an average depth of six inches, American enterprise can lose productivity because those who provide investment funds will no longer make discriminations at the margin, the significant choices. "I can't tell you," said Laszlo Birinyi, Jr., in 1988, while still at Salomon Brothers, "how long it's been since someone coming to work here told me he wanted to go into stock research."

Index funds are especially poisonous to the operation of a market because they lock up stock in impenetrable vaults until dramatic changes in the relationship of interest rates and corporate earnings trigger massive outflows. Birinyi argues that the arrival of the index fund has made the U.S. stock market more like that in Japan, where members of a *kereitsu* (formerly *zaibatsu*) group own most of each other's stock and never sell it. Yields on stock will thus tend to decrease over time. If true, this would over time have clearly deleterious effects on savings and investment.

My hunch, by contrast, is that the U.S. markets have become more like the Japanese because stock markets that move according to activity in indexes are driven essentially by changes in the liquidity of the banking system—that is, by the monetary policy of the central bank. The tendency has been exacerbated in the United States by the resolute commitment of the Securities and Exchange Commission to liquidity at all costs. More than half a century ago the study on broker/dealer segregation lanced that boil: "The prominence of the quality of liquidity increases the inclination, already too prevalent, of buyers of securities to think in terms of the appreciation of the value of the security rather than the promise of continued and substantial earnings. This inclination impairs the value of the market as an accurate barometer of investment opportunities and thus tends to vitiate the judgments of even those buyers who do think in terms of underlying worth."[21] (Remember that those words were written *in 1936*.) Because pension funds purchase index baskets according to formulas that compare returns on Treasury securities to returns on stocks, the money flows in as the Fed opens the spigot and whirlpools out as it pulls the plug—sabotaging not only the value of stock market prices as a guide to investments but also the effectiveness of monetary policy as a tool for control of the economy.

Other problems dealt with in these pages require attitude, cultural, or legal changes. This one is easier. A few formal market rules can rectify most of what does harm here. The European option, which can be exercised only on the date of its expiration, removes the possibility of using traded options to profit by manipulation in other markets: There's no point pushing the price today if you can't exercise the option for six more weeks. Giving the option a single exercise date also saves a lot of widows and orphans who don't live near Atlantic City or Las Vegas from blowing their inheritance in a casino. Meanwhile, the prohibition of cash-settlement futures contracts would limit the creation of such contracts to the perceived supply of the underlying "commodities." Other apparently intractable difficulties can be eliminated by the re-creation and extension of the old "time strike" rules that forbade people who handled a public order to trade that security or any derivative of it for their own account. Such rules would undoubtedly reduce trading, but that does not for a moment mean they would reduce real liquidity. And almost by definition, they would increase the supply of the patient money which is what the country needs.

CHAPTER 6

Fixed by Technology

All markets are information systems, but not all information systems are markets. When working properly, markets generate two items of information—price, and the dimensions of the interest in the security or commodity. Within the context of markets, information is what Vince Lombardi said about winning: It's not the most important thing, it's the only thing. Knowledge may be power elsewhere; information is power in a market. Technology changes the cost, distribution, validity, duration, and to some degree, the *nature* of information. Much of what has gone wrong in our markets is the result of accepting the advantages in cost and speed the new technologies have brought, without analyzing the changes they dictate in the day-to-day operations of the markets, in the relative status and power of the participants, and in the significance of the information the markets produce.

These changes are often unexpected, perhaps unpredictable. By rights, the most technologically sophisticated of all markets should be that for U.S. Treasury paper. Government bills, notes, and bonds have been "dematerialized" in the United States—they exist only in the form of book entries at the Federal Reserve Bank of New York (and in duplicate form at backup facilities in undisclosed locations). Ownership of the bonds that are bought is transferred immediately by the Fed from the seller's bank to the buyer's bank, and within the bank more or less immediately to the real purchaser. The money paid for the bonds is transferred at the same instant from the buyer's bank's account to the seller's bank's account, and within the seller's bank to the account of the real seller. These are markets for very big players: The minimum order is a million dollars, "and if you want to trade a hundred thousand dollars," said Gedale Horowitz, managing partner of Salomon Brothers and chairman of the Securities Industry Association, "they charge you extra; it's an odd lot." Everyone buys through dealers, and everyone is pretty much dependent on what the dealers say the prices are. There is no "tape" to report trades. *And there is no one screen where all the bids and offers are posted.*

Records of these transactions probably could not be kept by hand even if people wished to do so, because the number of transactions is too great. The daily volume of trading in governments is about twenty times the trading on the NYSE, by value. U.S. Treasury bonds and bills are the only "securities" truly traded around the clock, though people do have a chance to grab a bite of dinner between 6 P.M. New York time, when the Fed puts the West Coast out of the trading business by closing down FedWire everywhere in the country, and the opening of the Tokyo market at 9 P.M. New York time. If one includes government securities sold subject to repurchase agreements (which is a form of borrowing, not of trading), the total change in the ownership of Treasuries every day has been more than one hundred times the value of stocks sold on the NYSE. The face value of the T-bond and T-bill contracts traded on the Chicago exchanges (and on the London and Singapore exchanges, both of which trade futures in U.S. Treasuries) is seven or eight times the value of trading in the futures contracts on the S&P 500.

As of mid-1990, there were about eighteen hundred registered dealers in government bonds, but most of them were inactive. The only significant players in the game are a group of about forty "primary dealers" recognized by the Federal Reserve System, plus another ten or so that are candidates for that distinction but have not yet been "recognized." Virtually all the money-center banks are primary dealers, either through departments in the bank (regulated by the banking regulators) or through separately incorporated subsidiaries (regulated by the National Association of Securities Dealers or the New York Stock Exchange). All four of the big Japanese brokers and three of the big Japanese banks are primary dealers, as are the three big Swiss banks, Barclays and S.G. Warburg from Britain, and the ten largest U.S. brokerage houses.

The advantage of being a primary dealer is that the Federal Reserve Bank of New York, conducting the "open market" operations that are the instrument of monetary policy in the United States, will do all its buying from (or selling to) these primary dealers. This represents a lot of business, because the Fed continually adjusts its portfolio—buying T-bills to put reserves into the banking system and selling them to take reserves out, with the goal of maintaining a stable interest rate on the borrowings banks do from each other. Until late 1991, only primary dealers were permitted to bid for customers at the auctions when the Fed sold newly issued Treasury paper. The disadvantage is that primary dealers must keep the Fed informed of all their activities in the Treasuries markets and must stand ready to buy when the Fed wants to sell, or sell when the Fed wants to buy, "even during adverse market conditions."[1] As often happens in these markets, dealerships tend to be profitable when prices are rising (which means the value of the inventory is going up), and unprofitable when they are falling (the value of the inventory is going down).

But the Treasuries market is fragmented and secretive. "Trading in securities that are supposed to be the safest instruments," SEC chairman Breeden told Congress after the Salomon fiasco, "actually involves the greatest latitude for intermediaries to utilize improper sales practices."

Nevertheless, despite this concentration and the public nature of the instruments being traded, the Treasuries market has become the most fragmented and perhaps the most secretive market we have. The primary dealers do not trade with each other directly. Instead, they go through seven "interdealer brokers," each of which supplies screens to most of them, and (with one exception) to nobody else. These screens are crowded with information, because except in the futures market nobody trades "government bonds" as such. Bonds are issued four times a year by the Treasury, and each series is separately traded—the 8⅞s of November 1998, or the 13⅜s of August 2001, or the 7½s of May 2016 (the numbers refer to the year the bond will be repaid and to the percentage yield on each bond: A $10,000 bond at 8⅞ pays its owner $887.50 interest per year in two equal installments). Prices for the bonds are quoted in 32nds of a point, about $3 on a $10,000 bond. Rising interest rates mean falling bond prices; falling interest rates mean rising bond prices.

Typically, the interdealer screen will show the dozen most actively traded bonds, each described by its date and coupon rate, displaying a bid and asked for each bond, plus the "size" (the number of bonds) bid for and offered at those prices. The most actively traded bonds may trade at a spread of 1/64th (shown with a "+" after the number of 32nds), but the usual gap between the bid and the asked is 2/32nds or even 4/32nds, up to as much as a full point in issues that have less than fifteen years to run and trade rarely (issues that have more than fifteen years to run are eligible for delivery in satisfaction of the T-bond contract on the Chicago Board of Trade, and neither the bid nor the asked deviates far from the adjusted price that reflects their value for that purpose). The basic "benchmark" bond from which other valuations are derived is the most recently issued thirty-year Treasury. Though the interdealer brokers do business with fewer than fifty Fed-recognized dealers and candidate dealers, they are firms of good size, each with employees numbered in the hundreds and with more than five thousand screens in customers' trading rooms.

When a trade is made, the screen displays the price at which the bond was just bought and sold in a way that tells the subscribers a trade has just been done, with the quantity specified in millions of dollars of face value. At some interdealer brokers, the message is given by means of the word HIT (someone with bonds to sell has agreed to sell at the bid price) or TAK (someone has bought bonds at the offered price). At others the price begins to flash on and off. In either case, other dealers can now come in and trade at that price if they wish, and the number of millions of dollars of bonds traded can rise rapidly. I stood looking at a screen one day and watched what had started as a $6 million trade turn into $115 million at that price before my eyes. *Only the dealers who are watching this screen know that these trades are happening at these prices.* If there are no further takers for about twenty seconds, the screen returns to its normal bid-asked configuration—no HIT, no TAK, no flashing numbers.

It should be noted that the interdealer broker is not a specialist and never trades for his own account. He will not narrow the spreads by making bids himself. All the bids and offers on the screens have come from the dealers, and trades can occur only when one of the dealers hits the bid or takes the offer another dealer has given to the broker. Just as the interdealer brokers are not dealers, the primary dealers are not brokers: They buy from and sell to each other for the purpose of selling to or buying from their customers—the pension funds and money market mutuals and banks and bank trust departments—at a profit.

The primary dealers put their quotes on the brokers' screens by means of telephone calls. I visited one of the larger interdealer broker firms in spring 1991. No fewer than 140 brokers, nearly all of them young men, sat in a long, narrow trading room the width of a Wall Street building, behind tables that curved around in a series of crowded horseshoes (the largest of them built on steps), each horseshoe devoted to U.S. Treasury paper of a different duration. (The sign at the elevators showed arrows to "4s & 5s," "7s & 10s," "shorts," "longs," and "zeros.") The lights were dim. Each broker had his own telephone switchboard connecting him to anywhere from one to five dealers, with whom he talked all day long. His own screen showed him the prices of a range of bonds, but what he looked at was a pair of home movie screens that closed off the horseshoe, onto which overhead projectors beamed numbers (bids on the left-hand side, offers on the right). Each screen had eight or nine horizontal lines of numbers, each line representing one series of bills, notes, or bonds, written in grease pencil on a glassine sheet by one of two young women (called "peckers"—nobody remembers why) who sat in the center of the horseshoe listening to the numbers called out by the brokers along its rim.

Another young woman sat behind the peckers, punching with quick gestures at a keyboard, entering into a computer and thus into the customers' screens the prices written on the glassine sheets. She also had a button to push to indicate a trade when one broker called "Bought" or "Sold" to another. When brokers were making purchases or sales they stood up behind their places at the horseshoe and yelled. As the computer screen flashed the number at which the bonds had traded, the two brokers breathed into their telephones, to their dealer-customers, the single word "Done." Each bid, each offer, each hit or take came with a two-letter code that identified the dealer making it.

Most of the primary dealers use only three or four of the interdealer brokers, including one (Liberty Brokers) owned by the dealers themselves. Each of these brokers *is* in fact a separate market; bids, offers, and prices may indeed—normally will—vary a little from broker to broker, depending on which dealers call which brokers first. There is no central marketplace where discrepancies get smoothed away by "price discovery." Dealers usually monitor several screens, but not all of them, and they pay most attention to the broker with whom they place their own bids and offers. The dealers' customers do not know whether their dealer has got the best price—or whether the price being charged to them reflects a less-than-best price paid or received by the dealer. The customers do not have access to the interdealer broker screens and there is no tape to print the trades.

Whatever screen he buys from, the dealer does not know which competing firm sold to him or purchased from him. The interdealer broker is a "blind" broker. Only the interdealer broker himself has all the pieces of the puzzle, and he won't talk. The broker's computer tells the computer in the broker's bank to notify the purchaser's bank that one of its customers has bought X million of the January '02s, and the bank must pay the seller's bank X million dollars against delivery of the bonds, right now, by same day funds accessed through the Federal Reserve. At the same time, the broker's computer tells the computer in the seller's bank to transfer ownership of X million of the January '02s to the purchaser's bank, also right now, through the securities wire of the Federal Reserve. All government bonds, as noted, are represented by book entries at the Fed. Meanwhile, each bank's computer tells its own customer's computer that he is so many bonds or dollars richer, so many dollars or bonds poorer.

At no time in this process does the interdealer broker have

either the securities or the cash. He gets paid a commission by both sides of every trade (the rate is $39 per million dollars; only a few years ago the rate was $150 per million dollars of bonds, which contributed to a lot of riotous living by people who worked for bond dealers and accepted entertainment from bond brokers. Even at today's rates, the interdealer brokers are said to make $300 million a year[2]). The buyers have the bonds, courtesy of the banks and the Federal Reserve wire transfer system, but don't know from whom they bought them; sellers have the cash, through the same devices, but don't know who paid them. They also do not know what price other buyers and sellers may have paid or received for bonds at that time.

In 1989, a Government Securities Clearing Corporation was formed to permit the brokers and dealers to net these transactions, producing a printout that shows only the bonds each clearing bank has transferred to the Fed or must now transfer to the Clearing Corporation, and the money that has been or must now be paid. Because of the variety of different bonds, this system is not so smooth as other clearing operations, and has not displaced the separate clearings operated by the brokers themselves through the customers' banks.

The only interdealer broker that supplies quotes to the public is Cantor Fitzgerald Securities, lodged on the 105th floor of the World Trade Center. As long ago as 1969, Cantor launched a bond quote service called Telerate as an advertising service for its own dealership. When the securities house moved to the 105th floor it installed on the 104th floor what had become a computerized information service, much expanded to include news and quotations from other markets, foreign exchange rates and such, and services from information vendors who rent "pages" in the Telerate menu and charge Telerate customers separately for access to them. In 1989, Telerate was sold to Dow Jones & Co., publishers of *The Wall Street Journal*, but the service continued to supply the quotes from the Cantor Fitzgerald screens to anyone who wished to subscribe and would pay for the special PC and the telephone line plus a monthly fee. These quotes, however, were not quite as complete as the quotes offered to the primary dealers themselves—and were not in any event entirely authoritative, because each interdealer broker in effect runs a separate market in government bonds, and Cantor Fitzgerald can show only one market.

For trading purposes the screens displaying the quotes of individual interdealer brokers have more recently been partly displaced by a computer system developed by Michael Bloomberg, formerly a Salomon Brothers trader—chief of its equity department at age thirty-two—and now proprietor of Bloomberg Financial Information. With the help of Merrill Lynch, which owns 30 percent of the company, and until 1988 forbade Bloomberg to sell his services to any other of the twelve largest dealers, Bloomberg taps into three of the interdealer broker screens and displays the best bid and best offer from these three at that instant. The Bloomberg system also provides computerized analysis of the market and its trends, identifies the spreads between instruments of different lengths, and spots arbitrage opportunities among different bills, notes, and bonds. Bloomberg screens reporting on the relative values of corporate and municipal bonds, stocks, bank loans, currencies, and foreign bonds are available to anybody with the requisite $1,000 a month per screen to pay for them ($1,500 if one wants only one screen). But in the Treasuries market, the Bloomberg screens, like the interdealer broker screens, are available only to the forty-odd primary dealers and aspirants to that status.

Partly because of that restriction (though the primary dealers take thousands of screens), the governments market has become a relatively minor part of Bloomberg's service these days. The big call on him now is for corporate bond information and "analytics," the call coming from virtually all the institutions and the broker/dealer firms. At the close of every trading day, virtually all the major corporate bond traders and dealers supply Bloomberg with the prices at which different bonds sold that day. Overnight, the Bloomberg computers generate for each category of bond a "yield curve" reflecting the value of this sort of industrial or utility or transportation bond as a "zero-coupon" (a bond that keeps accumulating interest and pays everything at once on the date of maturity). Analyzing bonds as zero-coupon instruments permits easy comparison of bonds issued in different interest-rate environments. That's hard to do by hand, because it requires calculation of an "option" premium to reflect the fact that when a bond pays you a semiannual interest coupon you have various choices of what to do with the earnings. For each of Bloomberg's seven categories of bonds the computer establishes "Bloomberg Fair Value," against which a bond trader can measure the price he wishes to bid or ask for a specific bond in that category. The contribution here is quite similar to that made by the synthetic thirty-year Treasury bond traded at the Chicago Board of Trade: Suddenly purchasers and sellers of bonds can see through the fog of particularity to the actual movements of the market.

The push of another button on the Bloomberg console shows what any individual bond sold for yesterday (little "x" markings on a graph on the screen) by comparison with the "fair value" for its category, its rating within the category, and the historical record of how it usually sells with relation to other bonds in that category. The Bloomberg computers know which dealer or trader traded at which "X" on the screen, but the identity of the dealers supplying the information is never revealed to the public.

In this context, information on the prices of government bonds is most important as a way of setting the "fair value" yield curve for corporate obligations. Bloomberg has similar procedures, incidentally, for mortgage-backed securities, and is currently in the process of putting into his data base everything there is to know about some one and one-half million issues of municipal bonds. . . . Next stop, pricing the loans banks buy from and sell to each other in a market every bit as opaque (and therefore every bit as crooked) as the junk bond market.

As of spring 1991, Bloomberg had about fourteen thousand screens in offices around the world, with data-collecting centers in Tokyo and London as well as New York and Princeton, and he was selling new screens to customers at a rate of about five hundred a month. We are talking of a publishing enterprise that already has an income of more than $150 million a year, and is growing faster than anything that uses print. Bloomberg runs his own news service as well as the analytics and the prices—the only daily paper that keeps *one* reporter permanently on duty at the SEC, Bloomberg points out, is *The Wall Street Journal,* and he has two people stationed there all day, every day. (He also has access to and sometimes puts on his screen data from other news services from all over the world, including China and the Soviet Union.) His headquarters occupy three floors of the lovely Park Tower, perhaps the handsomest of New York's glass-sheathed office buildings, not on Wall Street but at 59th Street and Park Avenue.

In 1989, half a dozen of the biggest primary dealers announced that they would soon launch a new, totally computerized interdealer broker firm under the name EJV for "Electronic Joint Venture." This service would dispense with telephones, permitting dealers to place or hit bids and offers by speaking into a microphone built into the computer screen. Through a computer program developed by Verbex Voice Systems, the machine would learn to recognize the voice of each dealer using it, honoring only those commands uttered by a familiar acoustic pattern. Having recognized the voice, it would understand the command, display the quotes, and register the trades. For those using this system, commissions would be less than half those charged by the existing brokers. The real money in EJV would be made through the information service, which would carry to all investors the prices the dealers who own the system were paying and charging for government securities, on a real-time basis. Two years were required to develop this system, which came on-line as a partial service—short-term Treasury bills and notes only—in May 1991. In summer 1991, both its practicality and its acceptance by a market with no love for the big dealers remained uncertain.

What EJV has going for it is a growing demand in government for better information about the actual prices at which government securities change hands. In a report on the market in 1990, the General Accounting Office urged that the Treasury and the Federal Reserve find ways to ensure that participants in what is probably the most important market in the world, trading the greatest dollar volume of securities, receive greater access to what is really going on: "From an investor protection standpoint, the availability of transaction information from the interdealer screens will make it easier for more investors to become sophisticated in protecting their interest by being better able to evaluate the reasonableness of the prices quoted by dealers."[3]

The brokers themselves expect major changes. Some will be dictated by computer technology. (I described the firm I visited in the past tense because by the time these pages are published it expects to have eliminated its overhead projectors and movie screens and to have taught the peckers to enter quotes directly on their computer terminals.) Some changes will relate to the worldwide spread of trading in U.S. government securities. At least one of the brokers already has a staff reporting for work at 3:30 in the morning to do blind brokerage on bids and offers that in theory are being made in the London market but actually are available for trading in New York. Unfortunately, the Fed, which has no love for transparency in any financial market, remains content with the world as it is. And Michael Bloomberg, conscious from his Salomon days of how much goes on in other markets, cannot find it in his somewhat excitable heart to get worked up about the danger that somewhere an institution is paying two hundred and fifty-sixth of a point too much, or receiving two hundred and fifty-sixth of a point too little, when buying or selling Treasury paper.

Clarifying by Computer

Screen-based trading, which is supposed to take over from both floor trading and the sort of telephone-based trading we found at the interdealer brokers, first came to the securities market on February 8, 1971, when the National Association of Securities Dealers (NASD), over no small objection from its members, launched the first automated quote system, otherwise NASDAQ. NASD was and is the "self-regulatory organization" for securities brokers and dealers who are not members of exchanges. A private organization with public responsibilities, it was created subsequent to the passage of the Securities and Exchange Act of 1934 to enable the SEC to regulate, without getting into hands-on supervision, markets that were not exchange markets. Like the exchanges, it is owned by its members (any over-the-counter dealer registered with the SEC becomes a member), it establishes rules of trading (subject to SEC approval), and it disciplines members who break them. It also, like the exchanges, promotes the interests of its members with the public, the Congress, and the SEC itself.

NASD members trade mostly in securities that are not listed on an exchange. Only the largest corporations have ever had enough stockholders and enough recognition in the investment community to qualify for auction trading on an exchange. The stock of most companies has always traded, if at all, over-the-counter, through dealers who maintained inventories in these securities. Prior to 1978, dealers in over-the-counter stocks did not report their trades, and there was no public record of prices. There were published reports of what dealers were bidding and asking, put together by a private service called the National Quotations Bureau, owned and operated out of a five-story nineteenth-century merchant's building near the East River by a ramrod-straight elderly gentleman named Louis Walker. His daily book of about three hundred "sheets," yellow for bonds and pink for stocks, had some three thousand subscribers, all registered dealers (nobody could get a subscription without demonstrating to Walker that he was a registered dealer). About twenty-five hundred of them paid the extra thousand dollars or so a year to list their quotes as well as receive the publication.

This was all pretty informal. The quotes were gathered by a group of runners who visited dealers in New York, Chicago, and San Francisco and picked up envelopes at receptionists' desks. Because they were quotes offered at midday yesterday, nobody could be held to them today. Size was nominally a hundred shares—such matters could be discussed over the telephone when someone called to do business. I reported in my book *Wall Street: Men and Money* in 1955 that sizes tended to be larger for cheap stocks and smaller for expensive stocks, and God knows that may have been true. It was a simple time. Another group of Walker's people manned telephones every afternoon and called a sample of dealers to pick up retail quotes—what the dealers were charging their customers rather than each other. These retail quotes were then passed on to the NASD, which took the responsibility for getting them to the Associated Press, the United Press, and the six newspapers that took their duties seriously in this area. Donald Regan—later to be CEO of Merrill Lynch, Secretary of the Treasury, and chief of staff to Ronald Reagan, but then merely the boss of the Merrill over-the-counter trading department—said that the prices in the paper gave the public "nothing more than rough guidance."[4]

In 1964, the SEC's *Special Study* criticized the NASD for its failure to police the over-the-counter market, where price markups were often whatever the dealer could get away with and customers sometimes paid commission on top of the markup. The study recommended the appointment of a full-time president who would be a member of the organization's board of directors. (Previous presidents had been servants of boards on which they did not sit.) The first such was Robert Haack, who moved on to become president of the New York Stock Exchange. The second was a stockbroker from Cleveland named Gordon Macklin who had been serving on the board, a compact man with black hair and a misleadingly cynical smile, who arrived with the ambition to make the over-the-counter market a ponderable rival to the exchanges, capable of retaining listings that in past years would have moved to the auction market. The *Special Study* had argued that such retentions would be possible if the O-T-C community could improve trading conditions. The central requirement, clearly, was a system that would allow dealers to publicize their quotes and change them as rapidly as the bid and asked numbers changed on the floors of the exchanges.

This project was put into the hands of an NASD "automation committee," which engaged the consulting firm of Booz•Allen & Hamilton, which in turn prepared specifications that were put out for bid. Only one bid came in, from Bunker/Ramo, which raised the money for the project itself—the cost was $25 million in 1968 dollars—and housed it in a specially designed building in Trumbull, Connecticut. "We turned it on February 8, 1971," Macklin remembers fondly, "and lo and behold, it worked." Five years later, NASD bought it.

Once the larger dealers were on the system, the smaller dealers could not afford to be off. The main problem the first year was that dealers were unwilling to be bound by the quotes they put on the screen—after all, they hadn't been bound by the quotes they put in the pink sheet. A little persuasion, however, convinced the dealers that if the stock exchange specialists were bound by their quotes on the floor, the over-the-counter dealers had to be bound by their quotes on the screen. Macklin was concerned that the natural reaction would be to quote only for the first hundred shares, which, indeed, the dealers did. If the buyer or seller wanted to do more than one hundred shares, the dealer retained the right to haggle away from his price. Harry Keefe, largest of the bank stock dealers, convinced him not to worry about it. "One of my biggest customers," Keefe said, "is Mellon Bank. If they find out my bid is good for only one hundred shares, they'll rip my telephone line out of their switchboard."

To this day, most dealers list their size on the NASDAQ screen as 100 shares, but the NASD's Small Order Execution System (SOES) allows brokers to execute trades up to 1,000 shares (for 2,700 of the stocks traded) or 500 shares (for another 2,500) automatically, through the computer, at the price the dealer has put on the screen, without so much as the courtesy of a telephone call. The dealer finds out from his computer that he has just bought or sold shares. (No market-maker can quote only one side of the market: Every dealer who wishes to put buy quotes on the screen must also put sell quotes on the screen.) One of the first requirements of a computer program for an O-T-C dealer is that it constantly update the firm's inventory, which is controlled by outsiders.

As the name indicates (NASD Automated *Quote*), Macklin's machine was not at its inception a way to report trades. It was a computerized substitute for the pink sheets. In 1978, reacting to 1975 amendments to the Securities Act calling on the SEC to institute a "national market system," SEC Chairman Harold Williams began banging on Macklin and the NASD to report trades. Resistance to this innovation was heavy. "It meant," Macklin recalls, "that your customer knew your costs—if you'd bought twenty thousand shares at twenty, you couldn't charge him twenty and a quarter any more, you'd have to charge him twenty and an eighth, maybe even twenty and a sixteenth. But it gave much more credibility to the market to report the prices, and it helped retain companies that might otherwise have gone to the exchange." Because large transactions left the dealers with sizeable inventories or short positions, however, the NASD "tape" did not announce how much had been bought or sold at that price.

In the days of fixed commissions, a handful of well capitalized over-the-counter firms, most notably Weeden & Co., became significant figures in trading blocks of NYSE-listed stocks, because their markup was much less than the commission an NYSE member had to charge. This business pretty much went back to the member firms after commissions became negotiable, but the creation of the Intermarket Trading System in the 1980s—the exchange's and the SEC's response to a Congressional demand for a "national market"—opened the door to genuinely competitive order execution, not only on the regional exchanges but also by the O-T-C houses.

Bernard Madoff's is perhaps the most interesting O-T-C competitor to the exchange floor. A graying tough-talking maverick in his early fifties with a large nose and teddy bear cheeks, and with no great respect for his colleagues and competitors—though they elected him chairman of NASD in 1990—Madoff operates out of offices in architect Philip Johnson's unique "lipstick building" on Third Avenue, far from Wall Street. His fifty traders are occupied mostly in monitoring the firm's inventory on gorgeous orange-on-black, twenty-seven-inch square, backlit IBM screens (they cost $20,000 each), and hedging that inventory in the options and index markets, sometimes (about 10 percent of the time, laying off the position on the floor of the NYSE) to limit his risks on the billion-dollar inventory. Others put their bids on the NASD screen for one hundred shares, but Madoff's published size for the bids and offers to which he is committed is three thousand shares. But he is not a price-finder: His bids and offers are usually just "outside" the quotes others are putting on the screen.

A registered specialist in 450 of the 500 S&P stocks, Madoff has become a rival to the stock exchange as a market-maker. His promise to those who do business with him is that he will match the best price bid or offered on the Intermarket Trading System screen, and even if that price is there for only one hundred shares he will match it for three hundred. He does 4 or 5 percent of the daily volume in NYSE-listed stocks, which means almost 10 percent of the volume of trading by individuals. He has no public customers; he services only brokers, especially discount brokers. He probably does most of the Charles Schwab business, and he is the infrastructure that allows Schwab to advertise that when you call your Schwab customer's man he can tell you immediately that you bought or sold what you wanted to buy or sell and at what price. For this very valuable facility, Schwab pays Madoff nothing.

Indeed, Madoff pays Schwab for his orders—as he pays the other brokers who do a large volume with him—at a rate of 1¢ a share. "Volume," says Madoff, "is the life's blood of a dealer; why shouldn't I pay for it?"

Others do the same. In 1989, the NASD made a study of its membership, and found that 62 dealers making markets in listed stocks had made such payments to 241 O-T-C brokers who brought them orders from the public. If the customer wants to enter a limit order, however—to buy for less than the market price or sell for more—Madoff does not pay the broker for that, and half his volume is in limit orders, in part because he often gives a better service than the floor. If the market trades at the limit price, Madoff's customer makes the buy or the sale, regardless of whether the quotes show the existence of sellers or buyers at or near that price on the other side. On the other hand, Madoff's customers always buy at the offer or sell at the bid, while customers whose orders go to the floor may get a price that splits the difference.

The After-Hours Clubs

In 1987, the British news service Reuters bought Instinet, a computer-based brokerage service founded in 1970, a "fourth-market" system that specialized in matching buy and sell orders from institutions. Bids and offers were inserted anonymously, and until the trade was done a seller or buyer did not know the identity of the institution with which it had done business. The original appeal of the system was that the institutions would not have to go through their brokers to trade, in the days when fixed commissions made every transaction very expensive. Once negotiated commissions came on the scene, Instinet fell on hard times, and Reuters got it cheap. From its experience in the foreign exchange market, Reuters knew that the great attraction of Instinet was its anonymity, the opportunity it offered institutions to acquire or sell large positions without telling their brokers they were doing so.

Instinet was not, however, an efficient mechanism for "price discovery" or for negotiations. Increasingly, institutions wishing to minimize the impact of their trading on the market, and wishing also to report purchases and sales at the closing price printed in the paper, were arranging with their brokers to buy or sell "at the close," which might mean the actual execution of the order in the last five minutes of trading—or might mean the execution anywhere, including within the offices of the broker/dealer firm, at the closing price, after the market had closed. To meet this demand, while maintaining anonymity and eliminating the brokerage commission, Reuters launched "The Crossing Network" on the Instinet chassis, and put the marketing of the system in the hands of a Los Angeles-based consulting group called Plexus, headed by a matter-of-fact financial analyst and computer expert named Wayne Wagner, who advises institutions on the quality and cost of the executions they received from their brokers.

The Crossing Network offered institutions a chance to buy or sell at five o'clock New York time—one hour after the close of the market—at the closing price, any stock traded on the New York Stock Exchange or NASDAQ. The screen displayed the name of the stock and whether it was on bid or on offer, or both, but not the number of shares and not the name of the institution making the bid or offer. At five o'clock, bids and offers were matched, and the stocks parceled out pro rata by the computer (there was no specialist or market-maker to cure imbalances). The price was a 1¢ per share commission, and any large investor or trader with a high-quality credit rating could participate. Only one New York Stock Exchange member joined The Crossing Network, the specialist firm Agora Securities. Otherwise brokers remained ignorant of what their largest customers might be doing in the most actively traded stocks in the hour after the market closed.

There were occasions when the knowledge of what was happening on The Crossing Network could be of great value. On Friday, October 13, 1989, the market suffered its steepest one-hour decline in history, 190 points in the last sixty minutes, after the United Airlines leveraged buy-out deal collapsed and the gamblers who had been playing that stock with borrowed money had to sell everything else they owned to repay their margin loans on UAL. The 1987 crash had been in the record books for only two years. There could be no doubt that mutual funds would want to sell stock that afternoon through The Crossing Network, because they had to worry about demands for redemption over the weekend. The question was, had there been buyers—had stock traded on The Crossing Network at Friday's closing price? If it had, in any volume, then there wasn't too much to worry about when contemplating Monday: The nation's most important money managers thought they would do better picking up stock at Friday's close than they would if they waited for Monday's opening. If it hadn't, then it was storm-cellar time on Wall Street.

I was writing a column a month for the *Los Angeles Times* that fall, mostly about banks, and my editors there called. What should they do in covering the story of the collapse? I suggested that they check for activity on The Crossing Network. They tried; nobody would talk. So I tried on their behalf, and nobody would talk. Everybody was willing to give an opinion for publication about why the market had gone down or whether it would go down further on Monday, but the trading on The Crossing Network was information, and information that is worth money does not get given away to the press. In fairness, each participant on The Crossing Network knows only the business he himself has done, not the business done by others, but indicative information was circulating in that community. Some time later, after the information was no longer worth money, it was possible to learn that there had indeed been trading on The Crossing Network that Friday afternoon, and the market did stabilize fairly quickly on Monday.

In 1990, according to the Office of Technology Assessment of the Congress, Instinet, including The Crossing Network, was trading about 13 million shares a day, about 8 percent of the total volume on the New York Stock Exchange. Insiders say that about one-quarter of that was done on The Crossing Network.[5] Most days, it doesn't matter whether institutions are swapping shares in big corporations at what is already a known price, though technicians who base their analyses on volume are being deprived of what seems to them important information. On the days when it does matter, however, the loss of transparency is a direct violation of the intent of the Securities and Exchange Act of 1934.

In spring 1991, a computerized system for institutional trading that would permit prices to change after the market close was launched by R. Steven Wunsch, a personable, blue-eyed former manager of program trading for Kidder Peabody who won SEC approval for what he called an SPA (Single Price Auction). The system was alleged to run out of Wunsch's bedroom in one of the office buildings converted to residences across Nassau Street from the Federal Reserve fortress two blocks from the stock exchange. In fact, it ran on two supermini computers in Minneapolis, and the front and back office work of receiving the orders and clearing the transactions is done by Bankers Trust Brokers, an affiliate of the giant bank. What was in Wunsch's bedroom, as in that of many other traders, was a screen. By late 1991, the system was doing well enough to permit him to rent an office.

The Wunsch philosophy goes straight against the most cherished canons of trading and regulation in the United States, and against the dominant theories of the finance professors. Since all a market can do is fix a price at a moment in time, he does not see the purpose of continuous auctions, which rely on dealer accommodations to public demand. Intermediaries distort prices. The customer has the right to have a bid or offer go directly into the price discovery. Competing market-makers diffuse rather than increase liquidity, and round-the-clock trading is a terrible idea: "The more hours trading can take place, the more places it can happen, the less liquid the market will be," Wunsch says. "The image of the stock exchange specialist is bad, but what we are going to get will be very much worse. If the specialist doesn't have the order flow he's dead, and he's been losing the flow for thirty years." Transparency kills: "The worst market is the one where the order flow is constantly exposed. The market disappears though it's supposedly visible. The one thing the futures and derivatives markets have is that they centralize the flow—they don't allow upstairs trading."

What Wunsch offers is an automated version of the old "call" market, where one stock is traded at a time until a price is fixed for that time, and then the next stock is called to the attention of those in the market. This is still the way the options exchange opens every day, though it proceeds thereafter to a continuous auction. Wunsch at this writing has ten auctions a week, at 9:00 in the morning and at 5:00 in the afternoon Monday through Friday. The telephones open an hour before. On SPA's opening day in

April 1991, seventy-five institutions had filed to join but only fifteen had completed Bankers Trust's paperwork; by fall, Wunsch had forty-nine members. Any participant can put in a bid or an offer for what were on the first day any of 580 securities (by the end of 1991, the number was projected at something more than 2,000). The cost, paid only on completed trades, is from $1/2$¢ a share for entries in the first forty-five minutes to 1¢ a share for orders put in fifteen minutes before the auction to $6\frac{1}{4}$¢ per share for orders entered in the last twenty-three seconds. From the beginning, all orders are displayed, size and price, but not the identity of the orderer. An order can always be withdrawn, at double the commission chargeable for an order entered at the time of the withdrawal.

As the clock strikes auction time, Wunsch's computer draws the bids and offers for each stock as a demand curve and a supply curve out of the economics textbook, and if the two intersect, there is a price and a deal. Thanks to the minicomputers, all the stocks can trade simultaneously. Bidders who offered more than the equilibrium price find they have bought for less than they were prepared to spend; sellers who were willing to sell for less find they did better than they had expected; bidders below and sellers above the price are frozen out. And the market is automatically cleared, without intervention by a dealer. Everyone on the system knows which stocks traded at what prices in what volume, though nobody knows who bought and who sold (any more than anybody knows who bought and who sold a stock on the exchange). As of mid-1991, however, nobody not on the system was being told anything. The SEC could always get access to the numbers (though not the identities of the purchasers and sellers) through BT Brokers. To pay off the costs of developing the systems and buying and programming the computers (not to mention the legal expenses in seeing the thing through the regulatory process against objections from the NYSE and others), Wunsch figured he needed daily trading of two to three million shares, and he thought he would get it.

Instinet and Wunsch are by no means the only places where trading can be concealed. By Rule 390 of the New York Stock Exchange members may not make markets in listed securities in the United States off the floor, during or after hours. After-hours trading is done by some O-T-C houses, most notably Jefferies &

Co. in Los Angeles. There is a little trading of American equities in Tokyo after the sun has set in the United States, and a lot more in Europe, through mechanisms we shall look at presently, before the sun rises in the United States. As the exchange interprets the rules, member firms *can* trade in listed securities away from the floor in foreign countries, whether the customers are American or not.

Bernie Madoff, who has a substantial operation making markets for U.S. securities in London, says that his counterparts there are the big European institutions, but that most of the trading done by the other large U.S. houses in London represents "clean crosses" that firms like Salomon, Morgan, and Goldman have arranged between institutions that want to avoid the fees U.S. brokerage houses have to pay the exchange on each trade—and don't want to run the risk that the specialist for his own account or on behalf of his book of limit orders will break up their trade. The exchange says that most of the trading in London is by firms and customers that wish to escape the scrutiny of the market. A New York broker with a European clientele says there isn't any real "trading" of U.S. securities in Europe because nobody in Europe is interested in the European price of an American stock. Both are probably right. So is Wunsch, who says his system is going to make it "because the buy side is sick of London—the spread is worse and the liquidity is awful."

In June 1991, the New York Stock Exchange itself got into this game with a pair of postclose computerized trading sessions. The first simply duplicated The Crossing Network, except that the orders must be entered by member firms. There is some inducement to the member firms to use it to repair positions in intermarket trading, because the exchange has waived the up-tick rule for these trades. There isn't any up-tick rule in London, however, and it will be a great surprise to everybody, including the exchange, if this first postclose session gets used. (In its first two weeks, this session traded an average of 350,000 shares a day, against an average of about 25,000,000 shares an hour while the market was open.) The second session will involve only paired program orders involving at least fifteen stocks and a total price of $1 million. Here the exchange will waive its own fee and break its rule on reporting all trades. The stocks in the program will not be identified, although the price paid for the package will be announced at 5:15. The fact that this execution occurs on a computer rather than on the floor is irrelevant, except that it allows the people who work on the floor to go home the same time they always go home. This session got up a little over a million shares a day in its first two weeks of operation.

Enter CATS

NASD's advertising for itself proclaims "The Stock Market of Tomorrow, Today," and for a while in 1986 and 1987 it seemed that the NASDAQ system would become the model for securities trading, worldwide. The London Stock Exchange renamed itself the International Stock Exchange (this bit of braggadocio was reversed in 1991), and on the day of its famous Big Bang in October 1986 supplemented its traditional floor operations with screen trading through a system called SEAQ, for Stock Exchange Automated Quotations. Within two weeks, the floor had been closed forever, and all the trading was upstairs on SEAQ screens. None of this had been particularly well planned (a few weeks before Big Bang I asked Sir David Scholey, head of S. G. Warburg, whether the people in charge had thought through what they were doing, and he said, "No"). Government, academia, and industry alike trumpeted the promise of profits through mixing broking and dealing (formerly separate) and allowing the banks into the business of securities trading, with the predictable result that there was huge overcapacity in the business even before the bottom fell out on October 19, 1987.

Neither NASDAQ nor SEAQ behaved well in that emergency. Most dealers had never guaranteed the price on the screen for more than one hundred shares, and now it turned out that anyone who wanted to sell more than a single round lot was going to get a lot less for the stock. Richard Grasso of the New York Stock Exchange has been heard to complain that the market value of MCI, the communications company traded on NASDAQ, dropped by more than two billion dollars on trades of seven hundred shares. Dealers on both sides of the Atlantic had learned that the system could be "locked" by anyone who put in a bid that matched an offer, but didn't take the next step of executing the trade. Some dealers who were part of the Small Order Execution System (SOES) pulled the plug on the machine. In England, especially, dealers didn't pick up the telephone when it rang—quite apart from the fact that there weren't anywhere near enough telephone lines to handle the orders. After the self-congratulatory phase of postcrash analysis had ended ("we really did very well, considering"), NASDAQ took specific steps to remedy some of the weaknesses that had been exposed, especially by requiring dealers to continue to serve the SOES customers or give up their access to SOES business for at least thirty days after any episode of withdrawal from the market. In Britain, however, the situation deteriorated completely.

Because the screens gave publicity not only to the trades themselves but to the identity of the dealer who was bidding or offering for large quantities, significant transactions drew "cherry pickers," other dealers and brokers who would make life hard for anyone who had just acquired or shorted an order of significant size. Knowing a big trader had just bought heavily, the small trader could safely sell short, knowing there was a weight on the market of stock that had to be sold—or could safely buy against the big trader's short position, knowing big orders to buy were in the offing. This sort of gaming is much easier in Britain, where transactions don't settle until one whole week after the end of a two-week (or even three-week) "account period." All trading in the first part of an account period leaves the trader a week or more to reverse his trade without ever having to put a penny of his own money into it. By early 1989, the big dealers were threatening to do business off the exchange entirely unless they were permitted to withhold any public announcement of the price and size of their "bargains" at least until the next morning.

Further spread of the NASDAQ approach had already been dashed by early 1989, in any case, because the world had found a better mousetrap: Toronto's Computer Assisted Trading System, or CATS. NASDAQ is a quote-driven system: Markets move because market-makers change their quotes. At the New York Stock Exchange, not by rule but by evolution, there is only the one market-maker: the specialist at the post. Brokers doing business in NASDAQ stocks, however, will almost always have a choice of several market-makers—in actively traded stocks, more than several—all showing their wares on the screen. In this respect, the switch from trading floor to upstairs was less traumatic for the London Stock Exchange than it would be for New York, because London had always had two or three jobbers for each stock at different posts: The LSE was a leisurely place. Brokers could shop the floor for their customers, just as they can scan the screen for the NASDAQ/SEAQ dealer with whom they wish to do business.

As Steve Wunsch has noted, multiple market-makers are not necessarily an advantage for the customer. Brokers on the London floor, like brokers shopping the NASDAQ screens, might have all sorts of reasons, some of them quite irrelevant to the customer's needs, for preferring one dealer to another.

The Toronto system, by contrast, is an order-driven system. Brokers representing the public put bids on the screen as agents for their customers, and to the extent that an insider changes the price he or she does so by becoming a customer. By placing separate orders to buy and sell on the screen, any insider can in effect make markets the way the specialist does at the New York Stock Exchange or the dealer on the NASDAQ and SEAQ screens. (In theory, NYSE members can also "make markets" on the floor if the specialist's bid and asked are so far apart that they leave room for quotes in between them.) Indeed the Toronto Stock Exchange assigns a "registered trader" to do that in CATS stocks, in case public orders fail to produce transactions. The registered trader's purpose is to facilitate the execution of public orders, however, not to attract them. Orders can be partially filled, remaining on the screen at a reduced size.

The difference is subtle but real. The order in which bids and offers at the best prices come onto the screens is the order in which they are executed: "Time priority" is absolute, and nobody can play favorites. In this time priority schedule, the insider trading for his own account stands in the same queue as the outside customer. His order is executed precisely as it would have been had he been a dentist in Calgary looking to buy a few shares of Brascan. Because time takes priority, the screen simulates the gaming that occurs on a floor. The broker with 50,000 to sell must decide how much he wishes to put on the screen. If he offers all 50,000, he is assured that he will make the first sales to that amount at that price, but the fact that 50,000 are on offer may drive away buyers at that price. If he offers 10,000 and the offer is taken, he has to put his next offer at the end of the line of others willing to sell at this price—and by the time the market gets to him again, the price may be down. Dealers who see this coming, and jump in to sell against him, are vulnerable as they would be on the floor to a strategy which temporarily reverses gears and moves the bid up to trap the short sellers who are merely trying to ride on the original large order.

The original CATS was designed by a summer intern, a female math student with a temporary job at the TSE, and though the principles are very simple the computing machinery needed to make it work is rather intricate. The system was rolled out gradually, first in the relatively inactive stocks, then increasingly into the stocks that do the volume. In theory, trades can be effected and entered either from upstairs or from the totally wired trading floor the TSE built itself in the early 1980s as part of the modernization of downtown Toronto, and one does indeed see floor brokers at posts looking at screens. At the heart of CATS lies a degree of disclosure professionals have always felt to be impossible. The inside screen with the bids and offers *and sizes* is more widely available than the NASDAQ screen—and much more widely available than the interdealer broker screens. In 1989, the Toronto Exchange even made available to the public an aggregate screen, revealing the total bids and offers placed for a stock at each price up or down from the current quote. And in 1991, it dropped the other shoe, publishing the book of "limit orders" not only for the still-limited number of CATS stocks, but for everything traded on the TSE. The trading generated in Toronto by CATS is captured on a tape that reveals not only the price and size of each transaction but also the names of the brokers who did the trading. The tape is available from the exchange to anybody who will pay $100 a month for it.

Selling CATS to foreigners as a way to run an exchange has become a revenue source for the TSE. The system has been bought by all the French and Spanish exchanges, Belgium, and São Paulo in Brazil. The Paris Bourse had operated for centuries as a "call" market, with the list of stocks run through twice a day, in a morning session and an afternoon session, producing an auction that established a single price. As on the Wunsch system, customers who might have been prepared to pay more got their stock for less, and customers who might have accepted less got their stock for more.

When the Paris Bourse adopted CATS in 1984, it not only went to a continuous auction system but put all the bid and asked information—indeed, the aggregate screen—up on the satellite, for retrieval by anyone with a dish and a converter. The openness paid off with an immense expansion of trading—up nearly eight times between 1984 and 1989—though the development of sophisticated options and futures trading in the MATIF section of the Bourse doubtless contributed as much as the switch to CATS in getting traders. The French brokerage community, perhaps as a result, got in trouble in 1990, and volume was somewhat diminished in 1991. A study of the French market by a committee of insiders then recommended that "stockbrokers be allowed to trade large blocks of shares at privately agreed prices, rather than having to stick to official market prices for all types of deals."[6] But the French goverment, so far, has maintained its commitment to openness.

Around the World in Eighty Milliseconds

E. Pearce Bunting, the white-haired, grave chairman of the Toronto Stock Exchange, saw CATS as the system that could unite the world's securities markets in a world of round-the-clock trading. "The more people there are on comparable systems," he said, "the greater the opportunity for people to do business together." Several U.S. markets made arrangements in the 1980s to permit the Far East time zones to trade U.S. instruments during their own working hours. Concerned that trading in its bellwether T-bond futures contracts would move to Tokyo, the Chicago Board of Trade in 1987 began a night-trading session (the clerks manned telephone lines dedicated to trans-Pacific communication), and two years later added an early-morning session to compete with London's LIFFE (London International Financial Futures Exchange), which had flourished trading U.S. Treasuries as well as British "gilts" in its splendidly remodeled version of the city's ancient Merchants Exchange beside the Bank of England. The Chicago Mercantile Exchange in the mid-1980s developed a permanent link with Singapore to trade the Merc's contracts, and Sydney adopted the New York Commodities Exchange gold contract so that Australians could participate in that market without special cost.

Internationalization is by no means a new idea. Baron Paul Julius Reuter got his start by using the first underwater telegraph cable, between Dover and Calais, to carry news of prices on the London Exchange and the Paris Bourse. More than a century ago Friedrich Engels wrote: "The colossal extension of the means of transportation and communication—seagoing steamers, railroads, electric telegraphs, the Suez Canal—have [sic] made a real world market a fact. The former monopoly of England in industry has been matched by a number of competing industrial countries; infinitely greater and varied fields have been opened in all parts of the world for the investment of superfluous European capitals, so that it is far more distributed."[7]

Through the 1920s, the last hour of trading in London was much enlivened by reports of the action when the market opened on Wall Street. Commodity prices have long been linked worldwide, if only because importing countries always had a choice of the exporting countries to which they would give their business. Governments around the world got into bad habits of controlling or manipulating prices because they wanted to protect their consumers from rising prices (or their producers from falling prices) in corn, wheat, sugar, copper, silver, tin, or oil to be imported or exported.

Gold was the unit of account by which countries measured the value of their currency, and as early as the 1860s the United States proposed to prevent exchange fluctuations by establishing through international treaty a common gold content for the U.S. half-eagle (a $5 coin), the British pound, and a new 25-franc coin the French were prepared to mint for the purpose. The Paris Monetary Conference of 1867 approved the proposal by a vote of seventeen to two, but one of the dissenters was Britain, which was the end of that.[8] London was the center of the largest gold market, a twice-a-day single-price auction (or "fixing") still conducted by five brokers around a table in the Rothschild offices. In later years, two other significant gold markets grew up, one in Hong Kong and one in Zurich, but only because a single definition of a trading unit (the "Troy ounce") was agreed on.

Today three players, the Soviet government, the Singapore Monetary Authority, and the South African mining interests (known within the community as "the red man, the yellow man, and the black man") are the dominant figures in all the cash markets. In the 1970s, the gold futures contract in New York, and the options on that contract in Chicago, spawned an active cash market for gold in New York, too.

International markets in stocks were and are a different kettle of fish. Wheat and gold know no nationality. They can be shipped and do not change. Even the debt instruments of governments, denominated in currencies convertible to each other, are essentially what John Maynard Keynes called "titles to money," and can be abstracted in a way that removes their nationality for trading purposes. Shares of stock, however, have a juridical significance. The corporation is an institution that has different legal standing in different countries, and stockholders have different rights. Shares, as the name indicates, are the partial ownership of enterprises that in turn own land, employ people, and generate some piece of the gross national product. Governments will not be indifferent to how shares are traded, and who owns them. In the United States, only a handful of foreign corporations have provided the Securities and Exchange Commission with all the information American law finds necessary for the protection of investors. Shares of some other foreign corporations trade as "American Depository Receipts," or ADRs, and a trustee bank holds the actual shares that have been deposited in return for the ADRs. In fall 1991, grabbing for business, the SEC approved the trading of *broker-created* ADRs without the approval of the foreign company.

True international trading began, necessarily, with the provision of information internationally, and the date is 1964, when the Reuters news agency launched its first financial service to report prices from the European stock exchanges. A quarter of a century later, traditional news services produced only 5 percent of Reuters revenues, which were approaching the billion dollar a year mark; exchanges all over the world lived in fear that Reuters computer systems, hooked into broker/dealers through two hundred thousand screens, would supplant all the exchanges and dealing systems the industry had created and lived on.

Reuters began intruding on the world of exchanges with its Monitor Dealing Service in 1981. Before then, the Reuters Monitor had posted foreign exchange quotes from banks, which supplied them free of charge, as a basic advertising instrument, and dealers working from these screens picked up their telephones to trade with those whose quotes were best. This being a tight-knit if not small world, the telephone lines were usually dedicated to communications between two currency dealers.

Given free convertibility of currencies, foreign exchange pricing is an elaborate but ultimately simple exercise with three central influences: trade flows, capital flows, and relative interest rates. The real purchasers are buying or selling because they are doing business across currency lines, and wish to take the foreign exchange risk out of their transactions. A Japanese company selling VCRs to an American importer will invoice the buyer in dollars and wants to know how many yen it will receive for those dollars on the date the invoice is paid. The company can guarantee that number by making a forward contract to sell dollars for yen, the actual exchange to be made in, say, ninety days, when payment from the importer will arrive.

These transactions necessarily generate a vast amount of trading. The difference between the price of dollars in yen today and the price of dollars in yen in ninety days must be the difference in the ninety-day interest rates of the two currencies. If dollars can earn 10 percent a year and yen earn only 6 percent, then the price of dollars in yen at the end of ninety days must be 1 percent lower than it is today—no more and no less—or arbitrageurs can make a certain profit by covering forward contracts with current purchases and investments to be reversed ninety days later. Reuters Monitor services displayed the best prices for various currencies on various time horizons as submitted by the banks on the system. They were valued even beyond this brute information because "windows" on the screens allowed traders to see simultaneously the various elements that influenced currency prices for different delivery dates.

The addition of the dealing service permitted purchasers and sellers to do business with each other through their computer keyboards, switched to the desired seller and buyer not through the telephone company but through the Reuters computers. All dealing remained bilateral: Reuters did not offer a clearing or settlement service, and its computers did not keep records of the trades. Once buyer and seller had made contact with each other through the Reuters facility, their communication was as private as it had been on the telephone, though their own computers kept a record.

In the 1970s, the standardized futures contracts of the Chicago Mercantile Exchange had taken away most of the forward foreign exchange business the banks had always owned, because buying or selling on the Merc was so much less expensive. With the arrival of the Reuters dealing service in the 1980s, the banks got the business back. Bankers, after all, have a large information advantage in foreign exchange trading, because they can anticipate—may, indeed, know for sure—the future needs of their customers. Forex trading, moreover, was pretty nearly a twenty-four-hour business, because banks, exporters, and importers were active in all the time zones and wanted to meet their foreign exchange needs during the hours when they did their other business. The banks could and did "hand over the book" from trading operations in one country to trading operations in another as the earth turned on its diurnal round; the Merc's contract opened for trading at 8:00 A.M. Central Time and closed at 3:00 P.M.

In 1986, as the limitations on its Singapore link became increasingly apparent, the Merc began exploratory conversations with Reuters, looking to the creation of a screen-based trading system that could keep its contracts alive round the world and round the clock. Some clever fellow found the name "Globex." To prevent the community of traders from stoning the thing to death, everyone agreed that it would operate only during the hours the Merc was closed. During the traditional CME trading hours, anybody who wanted to buy or sell a Merc contract would have to direct his order to the floor to be processed through open outcry.

Reuters, meanwhile, had plunged some distance into work on the "Dealing 2000" system that would present much more information on the screen and permit traders to execute strategies, not just trades. It was inherent in the Dealing 2000 system that the Reuters computer would keep records of the trades, creating an audit trail that would permit some government regulator, looking through the files, to see what each bank had been doing. An audit trail, and a permanent record of who had bought what, would be an essential part of any Reuters/Merc partnership. The Commodities Futures Trading Commission might be a pal as well as a regulator to the Chicago markets, but there was no way any American government agency was going to permit the introduction of widely used market systems that did not include an audit trail.

As perfected (everybody hopes) in 1991, Globex will be a CATS-like system, entirely order-driven, priority to price (of course) and then to time of entry. The screens themselves will be available to everybody, but only members of the Merc will be able to enter orders to bid, offer, or purchase. Transactions will be made by hitting keys on a computer keyboard, and the machine will have the capacity to fill orders partially. If the first order in is for one contract, and the next is for one hundred contracts, and the order on the other side is for one hundred contracts, the little guy gets his order filled and the big guy buys only ninety-nine— and if the price then goes away from him, he has an order for a single contract that has not been filled.

The Globex screen will show both the public and members the last price at which a contract traded, and the current best bid and offer, both with aggregate quantities. Individual bids and offers will not appear, nor will buyer or seller know the identity of the trader on the other side until after the computer generates the confirmation. In these markets all contracts are with the clearing house; the creditworthiness of the counterparty is thus not at issue. One of the improvements Globex offers over current procedures is that floor members of an exchange will *not* be able to play favorites in their choices of people to do business with.

"On Day One, Minute One," says Jack Walsh, CME's executive on the case, "the contracts traded will be Japanese yen and Deutschemark, and then we will build on that." As of mid-1991, Day One seems most likely to occur in 1992, which is four years later than original projections. The problems have turned out to be much more difficult than originally foreseen. Some of the most interesting of them relate to the time priority. When these markets get busy, bids come thick and fast, and to arrange them by time of entry requires a very fast computer. The machine to be used does thirty-two million "microflops" per second, permitting the division of a second into literally thousands of pieces. Different players in the game are located at differing distances from the computer, and even at the speed of light a message running through wires (satellites are hopeless for this purpose) will take measurable milliseconds to arrive. All customers on the service will therefore be tagged with an acceleration factor to permit their orders to appear in the right sequence.

For the Merc, the pot of gold at the end of this rainbow is world trading in its S&P 500 contract; the barrier preventing the Chicago exchange from reaping its just reward is the limited hours for trading on the New York Stock Exchange. This barrier may not be entirely insuperable, for Reuters is already in the business of trading U.S. equities in London, in competition with the SEAQ International system operated by the London Stock Exchange. Of the six U.S. houses that make a market in a substantial number of U.S. stocks in London—First Boston, Goldman Sachs, Bernard Madoff, Morgan Stanley, Salomon, and Shearson—only Madoff still puts quotes in SEAQ, and even Madoff puts his quotes in the Reuters system first. Madoff, who was intimately involved in getting London to adopt the NASDAQ system, feels a kind of noblesse oblige toward SEAQ, and feels that Reuters gets the business for an ignoble reason. By contract, bids and offers dealers put on the SEAQ system are firm, and dealers using the system must in fact do business at those prices. On the Reuters screen, however, bids and offers are purely informational, and a dealer can change his mind when his telephone rings. It is also true that the SEAQ system creates a record of the trade, while the Reuters system does not. As in its foreign exchange system, Reuters takes its computer out of the loop as soon as the parties to the transaction make contact, and the information they wish to give the outside world about that contact (if any) is their business.

Some fraction of the business done in U.S. stocks in London (and Tokyo) is real business for real customers who plan to hold the stocks for a while. German and Swiss banks, like Japanese life insurance companies, buy and sell American equities as an asset-diversification strategy, not as a trading strategy, and they want to do it at four in the morning New York time because that's when they conduct business. One experienced international broker says the totals are trivial, because whenever there is news about a stock, you can't really do business at the posted price if you're bidding or offering abroad. For London branches of New York securities houses, London offers an opportunity to serve institutional clients and to execute proprietary trading strategies without anything printing on any tape. If the SEC wanted to find out what these firms were doing, it could, because all the records of a U.S. registered broker/dealer can be subpoenaed through the main office. But there is also that shadowy market in London, however, conducted by British broker/dealer firms that do not have to show their blotters to foreign regulators.

James L. Cochrane, chief economist of the New York Stock Exchange, sees a future when truly international equity trading will occur. Companies want their stock traded in countries other than their home country, especially countries where they do business. Foreign stock ownership enables them to tap new capital markets, gives them, says Cochrane, "host-country currency pools for acquisition purposes," and makes it possible for them "to offer equity incentives, denominated in local currency, for host-country employees."

Cochrane, speaking to a *Financial Times* conference in London in April 1991, saw three possible scenarios for the creation of active cross-border markets in the last decade of this millennium. "One path to the future," he said,

is development and adaptation of home markets. . . . [T]he basic market for Disney stock would remain in New York. We would adapt to the off-hour (to us) trading needs of the world. Our job would be to find ways to make it easier for someone in Madrid to trade Disney stock in New York at 3 A.M. our time. . . .

The second approach is . . . "passing the book" through the time zones. By passing the book, I mean that major U.S. names would be traded in Europe during your business hours. When you're winding down, the book would be passed to New York. When we go home at the end of the day, the book would be passed again, perhaps to Tokyo. There would be twenty-four-hour trading, but the "book" and the liquidity in the stock would rotate through the time zones. One side benefit about passing the book would be that many clearance and settlement problems could be finessed because most trading would be done by investors in their home markets during their home trading hours.

The third path to the future is the emergence of "global vendors" . . . an environment in 1999 in which a person located anywhere in the world, at any time, seven days a week, who wants to trade shares simply calls a vendor. The vendors might have names such as AT&T Securities, BZW [Barclays Bank], Nomura, Merrill Lynch and Reuters.

Securities trading through vendors, Cochrane suggested, "causes many securities industry regulators to have restless nights."[9] And justly so, for the locus of such markets for legal purposes could easily be Jersey or Lichtenstein or the Cayman Islands. The United States, however, does not have to give what is politely called "comity" to the laws of such places or accept what is almost as politely called "regulatory arbitrage"—and there is increasing evidence that the European Community countries do not wish to set themselves up for such competition. The fate of our markets is not in our stars nor in the technological achievements of the information vendors. It is ultimately in our political will, our understanding of what markets and the participants in them do, and our ability to conceptualize the markets we want.

CHAPTER 7

The Vanishing Government

In the middle 1960s, the Los Angeles branch of the Wall Street house of Shearson Hammill got involved with United States Automatic Merchandising Company, in essence a jobbing firm that placed vending machines in factories. One of the officers of the branch became a director of USAMCO, and the firm became underwriter for an initial public offering of the company's stock. What followed was grimly described a few years later by University of Connecticut law professor Nicholas Wolfson:

> Employees of the underwriter held a substantial equity position in the issue after the offering. They had an obvious interest in maintaining the price of the stock until they could unload their holdings. . . .
>
> Shearson emerged as the dominant market maker in the stock and was both the primary wholesale and retail dealer. . . . Several months later the Shearson employees and partners who held USAMCO stock discovered to their consternation that demand was insufficient to cover their public sales. A "workout" market was immediately established, involving the following scenario:

No sell orders from customers were accepted unless offsetting buy orders were in hand.

Although Shearson continued to publish bid and ask quotations, these bids were phony, because Shearson had no intention of purchasing USAMCO from other broker-dealers.

Shearson employees solicited customers' bid orders. While they did this, they continued to quote Shearson's phony bid and ask quotes.

Partners and employees of Shearson sold their holdings of USAMCO to retail customers, even though prior sell orders of retail customers remained unexecuted.

Several of these unexecuted sell orders had been entered at floor prices *lower* than those the Shearson employees received in their sell orders.

Shearson employees advised retail customers not to sell their USAMCO holdings.

After the Shearson insiders unloaded their holdings, the manipulative workout market ended, and the price of the stock plunged. The Shearson customers who still owned the firm were badly stung.[1]

In the aftermath of this swindle, the Securities and Exchange Commission ordered the specific individuals involved out of the securities business forever, imposed a fine on Shearson Hammill— and with their consent punished the chairman and president of Shearson with a thirty-day suspension of their license to work in the securities business.

The president of Shearson at that time was Robert Van Tuyl, my friend and neighbor in the summer community of Shelter Island. He spent much of the time of his suspension on the island, in perfectly terrible mental condition. A hearty, cheerful man with a towering social background—the family name was van Tuyl van Serooskirken, that of a Dutch noble family; his ancestors had been in New York since the days of Peter Stuyvesant; his father was principal of DeWitt Clinton High School at the turn of the century, when that job was the equivalent of a college presidency—Bob had never imagined that he would see his name in the paper in connection with quasi-criminal activity. The firm itself was of such standing that the name survived after Sandy Weill put together, first for himself and then for American Express, an organization that combined his own firm of Cogan Berlind

Weill and Levitt with Loeb Rhoades, Shearson, Hayden Stone, E. F. Hutton, and Lehman Brothers.

Van Tuyl had not owned a share of USAMCO, and had never known about, let alone approved, the activities of the Los Angeles office. During the month that Van Tuyl was in purgatory, however, he never once complained that it was unfair for him to be punished for the activities of his subordinates. He was the chief operating officer of the company. He should have known; the shenanigans had happened on his watch. It was of the essence of being an executive that you took some of the credit and some of the responsibility for the repeated and continuing activities of your subordinates.

From 1978 to 1983, frauds of somewhat lesser but not entirely dissimilar character were perpetrated on the customers of the San Francisco office of Merrill Lynch, by a customer's man much admired in that office as one of its biggest producers. More than thirty-five complaints were filed against this salesman by customers—school principals, retired businessmen, nurses—who had lost their life savings following his investment advice. Merrill paid out $75,000 to some of the customers to shut them up, and defended lawsuits and arbitration procedures brought by other customers. Finally the San Francisco office of the SEC caught up with the swindle, and asked Washington for permission to bring charges against the brokerage house.

The chairman of the Securities and Exchange Commission when this case arrived in Washington was John Shad, a dyspeptic, jowly, self-important Utah broker—a Harvard MBA and a Shearson alumnus—who had been vice-chairman of E. F. Hutton in the days when that firm was kiting checks and putting its retail customers into situations that benefitted the firm far more than the customers. In 1980, the $39.4 million Hutton made by selling its own fancy tax-shelter deals, many of which would later rebound against the buyers, exceeded the firm's total profits of $37.3 million.[2] Shad had become chairman of the SEC because he was a large contributor to the Reagan campaign, and the Reagan White House could not think of anything else to do with him. Among his earliest actions as chairman was to relax capital requirements for brokerage houses to encourage them to do more trading for their own account (he made a speech a month or two into his tenure that what really ailed the nation's financial markets was the fact that brokerage houses were insufficiently profitable). Hutton wanted to advertise that its own open-ended mutual funds cost you nothing to buy; you just had to pay a "contingent deferred sales load" when you redeemed the shares. This had not been permitted under previous rules; Shad's SEC gave Hutton an exemption.[3]

In the Merrill matter, the SEC staff wanted to *fine* the firm and censure it verbally—in a business where everyone knows that only sticks and stones do any damage—for permitting what was obviously crooked behavior to persist in its San Francisco branch. No individual in Merrill corporate management would be punished in any way. Shad pushed the staff not to proceed against the firm, and when they went ahead anyway, he lobbied his fellow commissioners to reject the staff recommendation. According to David A. Vise and Steve Coll of *The Washington Post,* he said "it was unfair to charge a Wall Street House for bad deeds by an individual broker because other firms would use the negative publicity to steal clients."[4] Eventually, Shad voted against taking action against Merrill nationally on the grounds that, after all, these firms are so big these days, you can't really hold the boss responsible for what his underlings do.

One can hardly imagine a more succinct statement of what has gone wrong in our society. The essence of justice is that people should pay for what they break; the essence of office is that leaders should pay, at least in reputation, for what their subordinates break, especially if the accidents are profitable and frequent. Later Shad would use some of the profits he had earned during his days as an officer and shareholder in E. F. Hutton to endow a chair in ethics, no less, at the Harvard Business School, and Harvard would take the money. Still later, he offered his prestige as a former SEC chairman to Drexel Burnham and became its chairman in its last year as it tottered toward an insolvency created by flamboyant violation of the rules of fair trading through the years when Shad was at the SEC.

This is one of the irremediable losses suffered when professional service firms become corporations: People are no longer "partners," nobody is responsible, even with a touch of personal shame, for the activities of anyone else in the organization.

Juridically, corporations are separate from the people who work in them. For this reason, historically, governments have regulated the operations of corporations much more directly and carefully than the activities of partnerships. Self-regulation assumed collegial codes that governed behavior. In the 1980s, however, as these codes disappeared, victims of an emerging philosophy that anything that made money was okay as long as you couldn't go to jail for it, government actually reduced the extent of its oversight.

After all, these were big organizations doing business with each other. Big organizations, Shad insisted, were run by reputable, trustworthy people. Moreover, big organizations could take care of themselves, and didn't need government regulators to help them. The doctrine of corporate personality now came full circle, and was used to conceal the fact that the people who work within a corporation are inescapably part of it, even when its interests are by no means identical with theirs. Corporate ethics, like government ethics, is an oxymoron: Only individuals can feel ethical concerns. The corporation can brush away the ethical concerns of its employees with the whisk of a memo.

The 1980s, moreover, were a time when one of the crusades of the postwar era came to triumph—and produced the sack of Constantinople rather than the liberation of Jerusalem. As a water-carrier in the ranks in the early days of the crusade, I feel a particular revulsion at the results. What troubled those of us who started down this path in the 1960s was the economic illiteracy of the lawyers who had exclusive control of the courts and constituted by far the largest cadre of our legislators and of the commissioners and regulators in the administrative agencies. To gain relatively trivial goals they made decisions that had far-reaching effects on the operations of productive enterprises. Worse, they established goals that could not and would not be met, provoking cynicism and evasion of the law.

In the Congress, clean-air quality standards were set for Los Angeles and New York that could not be met without major technological breakthroughs or economic collapse. Affirmative action "targets" (never, of course, quotas) were established without reference to the size of the pool of trained black candidates. Zoning laws added hugely to the cost of housing to achieve slight improvements in health or safety or aesthetic value.

The social security laws were amended accidentally to provide retirees with additional benefits for *both* increases in the cost of living and increases in the average wage, which no one had intended—but for ten years it was impossible to correct what had been a drafting error.

Deregulation, a slogan in the Carter administration when the Cornell economist Alfred Kahn was head of the Federal Aviation Authority, became a shibboleth in the Reagan administration, whether the benefits claimed for it were likely or not. Nor was any help to be expected from the left. The concepts of cost and benefit were almost entirely foreign to the cadres of social revolutionaries who strongly influenced our media and academies in the 1960s. I wrote a book in the 1970s about the need to adjust law and public policy so that they related productively to the underlying trends in American society.[5] Professor Henry Manne of the University of Rochester started a foundation to hold seminars that would educate judges on the economic footings of the decisions they had to make. Gradually, the staffs in the White House, Congress, and especially the administrative agencies opened to economists.

Mostly, however—especially but not only at the SEC—they opened to finance economists. This was unfortunate, for finance economics is not economics. Translating from the Greek original, teachers used to define economics as the study of the allocation of scarce means to alternative uses. Common speech retains from the same root the word "economical." The two schools of economics dominant in this century trace back to the Englishman Alfred Marshall (represented by John Maynard Keynes) and the Austrian Eugen Böhm-Bawerk (represented by Joseph Schumpeter). Necessarily, in the circumstances they were trying to explain, they were business cycle theorists; they dealt with the impact of the past on the present, and with the likely results in the future of the policies pursued today. Schumpeter's early work stressed the concept of a "circular flow," in which one period's inputs created the next period's outputs, which then fed back into an input stream. His Harvard friend Wassily Leontief took this concept beyond theory to the development of an "input/output grid" to explain present economic conditions and indicate remedies.

Finance economics, by contrast, is about making money. It says nothing about the allocation of resources, or, indeed, about choice, the central concept not only of economics but of all social science. Finance economics teaches the necessity for diversification rather than choice, because diversification maximizes "risk-adjusted returns." Equity and debt must be exactly equivalent, because the market automatically equilibrates interest rates and expected capital gains, applying the appropriate tax benefits.

Finance economists are not monetary economists, though the latter have usually trained the former. A Chicago school monetary economist like Milton Friedman sees the artifice of money as central to the course of economic activity in a modern society created by the division of labor; a Keynesian monetary economist like Hyman Minsky sees financial instability as the source of instability in the real economy. Friedman finds the results and the verification of his analysis by correlations that posit time lags of considerable duration, and Minsky's analysis looks to balance-sheet deterioration and improvement over time. Finance economists by contrast live in a world of atomized transactions each of which has a "bottom line," after which the players begin the game again as though nothing has happened. "Expectations," not real gains and losses, determine behavior. It is a grubby, briefly useful, but ultimately ludicrous way to look at reality.

The community of finance economists has been very well supported by fund managers and investment houses. Where they find resistance to their theories, most of them react rather nastily. It is the finance economists who have spawned the theory of "public choice," which holds that government officials act to maximize their own income, not for the public good. It never occurs to them that the source of their own sponsorships may be the strongest influence on their theories.

The eruption of finance economics into the decision-making levels of the SEC has corrupted the agency's sense of purpose. If markets exist merely to enrich those who participate, which is the central message of finance, then the doctrine James Tobin has described as socializing losses and privatizing gains makes perfect sense. Rules that impede the maximization of profit must create greater costs than benefits, because maximized profit most benefits society. Behavior is always predictable, governed by the simplest tenets of sociobiology, and does not change significantly in conditions of stress or relaxation. The seventeenth-century philosopher Gottfried Leibniz proved long ago that this is the best of all possible worlds, making himself the ancestor of finance economics. One hundred and fifty years later, the British philosopher F. H. Bradley added the corollary that everything in the best of all possible worlds is by definition a necessary evil. He was the ancestor of the rest of us.

Perhaps the 1990s will be better. Certainly the top dogs at Salomon were made to pay for the greedy negligence with which they contemplated their firm's trickery in the Treasury auctions.

You Want It? You Got It!

One can illustrate the large things that went wrong at Shad's SEC with a small thing. Among the technical items written into the Securities and Exchange Act of 1934 was a prohibition against specialists taking discretionary orders. Such orders had obviously been abused in putting together the "pools" that drove prices first in one direction and then in the other to cheat public customers lured by original activity in a stock. Even when nobody was cheating, they put the specialist in an uncomfortably ambiguous situation.

Brokers have always left with specialists (because brokers can't make a living by hanging around a post and waiting for something to happen) "limit" orders from their customers that cannot be executed in the crowd at a particular moment. That's the "book" that presumably gives the specialist the information he needs to set opening prices and react to sudden price movements. Such orders are automatically activated when a stock sells at the limit price. Some orders are left because people are acquiring or disposing of stock, and wish to buy on weakness or sell on strength: With the market at 30, investors following such strategies will leave orders to buy at 27 or sell at 32. Others are entered as "stop loss" orders by speculators, who are willing to buy at 30 but would want to sell at 27, or are willing to sell at 30 but would want to buy at 33. This looks crazy, but it isn't. Essentially, what the speculator is saying is that if the market for a stock moves against him he is willing to admit he was wrong and get out before he loses more. That decision has to be made at the moment the stock is bought or sold, because the speculator knows that if he has to make it later he can't trust himself not to rationalize what has happened and hope for the best. The central difference between the market professional and the sheep in to be sheared is the professional's ability to take his losses.

Brokers as the agents of their customers have always been permitted to take orders that are "not held," which means that the man on the floor has the authority to decide that he'll be able to buy or sell at a better price if he waits a while. That, indeed, is the art of the floor broker, who gets his customer "the best execution." If his judgment is good, he gets more business, and may well be able to charge a larger commission. (In a world where the tick is 12½¢, a man who can save his customer a single tick is obviously an asset at 10¢ a share; the best brokers, working patiently over time, save their customers considerably more than a single tick.) The specialist, however, is not at heart the customer's agent: He is first of all a trader for his own account. Recognition of the difference between the broker and dealer functions may atrophy elsewhere, but it cannot die at the specialist's post.

Thus the specialist cannot take "not held" orders. He already has an edge on other people because he knows that there is demand for the stock at 27 (limit orders being more common than stop-loss orders), and even heavier demand at 26. If he can use that order to replace his own money the first time the stock sells at 27, however, he will be under terrible temptation to lighten his own inventory if the market is heading down, or increase it if the market is heading up, by using the customer's order to make the first transaction at that price. What the law says, then, is that the specialist cannot activate the limit orders in his book until there has already been a trade at the limit price.

In 1977, the exchange, with the permission of a Democratic SEC chaired by Harold Williams, permitted one partial exception to the rule, permitting occasional conversion of "percentage orders," orders that allowed (but by their nature could not command) a specialist to take for the customer's account, say, half the trades at the price specified by the limit or stop-loss order. This exception was narrowly circumscribed, because it permitted the specialist to determine the *size* of the trade in question. The percentage order became a market order only when the specialist "elected" it. This election was considered to be automatic after the market had traded at the price specified in the order, but before the 1977 ruling it had been forbidden until that moment, to make sure that the specialist could not elect at his discretion.

Under the terms of the 1977 rule change, the specialist was allowed to take a percentage order into the auction at the post the first time its price was touched, provided that the transaction was on an up-tick for sales or a down-tick for purchases. If the previous sale at a different price had been at 27⅛, the specialist could convert a percentage purchase order at 27 because that would help support the market. But he could not execute a stop-loss sale order at 27, because by absorbing buy orders this stop-loss order would help push the stock down—possibly to the disadvantage of the customer who had placed the stop-loss order, and who after all did not want to see the stock get down there. Finally, the exchange rule commanded that the counterparty in the trade could not be the specialist himself—percentage orders could be converted only to fill customer orders on the other side.

In 1983, the New York Stock Exchange asked the SEC for permission to authorize specialists to "convert and parity" these percentage limit orders, turning them into market orders the first time the stock sold at the limit price, *even on destabilizing ticks*, and to permit the specialist to be the counterparty on such trades, buying for or selling from his own book. The restrictions now related only to the size of the trade (10,000 shares or more), and the extent of the drop or rise from the price of the last sale (no more than one-quarter of a point).

This relaxation of the rule against conversion of percentage orders was part of a drive to let specialists continue operating on the floor with much less capital in relation to their volume of trading than would have been required in previous years. Shad's SEC two years before had lowered the capital standards for brokerage firms dealing with the public, and had in effect suspended the Federal Reserve's rule limiting the use of borrowed funds by broker/dealers.

Federal Reserve System Regulation T and Regulation U, controlling margin credit for the purpose of holding stocks, had always given a blanket exemption for market-makers, who were allowed to borrow on "good faith margin"—that is, whatever the banks would lend them. Broker/dealers qualified for exemption from Reg T and Reg U by filing an affidavit with the SEC stating that they were market-makers *somewhere*. On the New York Stock Exchange, only the specialists could be market-makers, but other exchanges were more relaxed about permitting brokers to call themselves market-makers. As the decade wore on, speculators— in the form of "risk arbitrageurs" who were playing games in the stocks of companies involved in announced takeover plans— needed increasingly large supplies of credit to carry their positions. They were not in any meaningful sense market-makers, but Ivan Boesky, their peerless leader, had found that he could make a claim to such status by acquiring a seat on a regional exchange where these stocks were or could be traded. Such exchanges had always been held to less rigid rules than those applied to the New York exchanges, because the SEC had always had a policy of encouraging competitive markets. The risk arbitrageurs could then claim exemption from Fed margin regulations.

The problem for Boesky and his clan was that the affidavit claiming market-maker status created an audit trail that might eventually be dangerous (after all, they were *not* market-makers). In 1982, therefore, on the grounds that nobody ever looked at these affidavits anyway, the SEC abolished the requirement that they be filed. Risk arbitrageurs then could and did go to their banks (where they were good customers) and on their unsworn and unsubstantiated claim to be market-makers could borrow as much money as some idiot of a banker would lend them. The Brady Report on the 1987 market crash noted (in a comment that privately shocked the responsible people at the Fed) that "professionals are not subject to the 50 percent margin requirement applicable to individuals. Professionals can invest in stocks on 20 percent to 25 percent margin."[6]

It should be noted that this danger persists, though the banks have at least temporarily learned that credit judgment is important. If John Reed of Citibank had known in spring 1988 what he told Citicorp's board in winter 1991—that the takeover of Federated Department Stores would bankrupt his client Campeau and wreck a number of bondholders—and had withdrawn Citibank's support for that atrocious deal, $4 billion of credit to risk arbitrageurs would have gone out of the market in a whoosh, creating a market break that might well have been worse than that of 1987. Indeed, something not far off that credit collapse knocked almost two hundred Dow points off the market in less than an hour on October 13, 1989, when Citi and Chemical had to admit that they could not put together the financing for a United Airlines deal that had pushed the market for its stock to somewhere between two and three times its real value.

When the NYSE proposed to relax the rules on specialists' execution of percentage orders, in part to allow specialists to enlarge the trading they could do with their limited capital, the SEC staff, already reduced by Shad both in numbers and in will to regulate, roused themselves for a last stand. In their statement to the commission, they pointed out that what the Stock Exchange wanted to do was prohibited not just by some regulation passed by some previous commission but by the Securities Exchange Act itself. Indeed, Congress in 1975 had strengthened the wording of the section, supplying a new legislative history specifying that the section was intended "to limit the activity of a specialist to that of a broker *or* a dealer . . . to eliminate conflicts of interest attributable to a combination of dealer and broker functions (e.g., acting as principal and agent in the same transaction)."[7] As amended, the act declared it "unlawful for a specialist permitted to act as a broker and dealer to effect on the exchange as broker any transaction except upon a market or limited price order."[8]

The Stock Exchange brief by Milbank Tweed Hadley & McCloy is a classic and excellent example of grumbling and kvetching and raising straw men to avoid the clear intent of the law. (It quotes a "former president" of the exchange extensively to support the law firm's version of what the 1934 Act terminology really meant; the staff reply noted that this president was the crook Richard Whitney, who went to jail for stealing from the exchange's pension fund, and that Milbank Tweed had got the exchange as a client at that time because its predecessor had been too tight with Whitney.) At the oral argument, the Milbank firm urged the commissioners "not to fall into the trap of the black letter law." They didn't: In 1987, they gave the exchange the go-ahead.

As a policy matter, the Convert and Parity (CAP) issue was not clear-cut. In the early 1970s, when the commission and the Congress worried about the structural problems growing out of the domination of the market by institutions—problems we shall be discussing in the final chapter—the staff had produced an anonymous and undated report on "Regulation of Trading on National Securities Exchanges." The report opened with the observation that undesirable changes in trading practices had occurred because of "the disparity among exchanges concerning membership requirements and the regulation of member firm trading, both on and off the floor." Regional exchanges, the report noted, had been exempted from the rules written "to insure that in all dealing by members for their own account, the interests of the markets and of the investing public are placed ahead of the interests of the members." As a result of these exemptions, "specialized markets have developed for trading by institutions on some of these exchanges which have more liberal rules in such areas as give-ups, reciprocal and rebative practices, institutional membership and other matters which affect the industry as a whole. Furthermore, substantial changes have occurred in market practices of members and member firms." The commission should act, the report concluded, "to avoid the possibility that the investing public will be irreparably harmed through the development of specialized professional markets providing special advantages to certain classes of exchange members."

The problems of "give-ups, reciprocal and rebative practices" were related to the fixed commission schedule then in force. Because institutions had to pay so much more in commission than the actual costs of servicing their trades, there was a great quantity of money on the table to be allocated by the money managers (sometimes, if the money managers were asleep at the switch, by the brokers). Many of these issues had been brought to a head by the willingness of the regional exchanges to sell seats to mutual funds and pension fund managers, who could then handle the entire process themselves, for their own benefit or for the benefit of the shareholders in the mutual funds and the pensioners (or the corporations that owed the pensions). In 1973, a distinguished advisory committee (its members included Alan Greenspan, Jack Nash of Oppenheimer, and Ralph Saul, later to be chairman of the American Stock Exchange) advised the SEC that whatever changes were to be made in stock trading procedures to create a "central market system . . . should not detract from the agency function of stock brokerage nor depreciate the value of having a broker act for a customer in handling purchases and sales of securities."[9]

In 1974, the SEC decided that allowing institutions to be members of exchanges and use those memberships to trade for their own account would violate the intent of the Securities Exchange Act. To prevent members from abusing their memberships for self-interest, the commission under Bill Casey's chairmanship proposed Rule 19b-2, requiring all members of securities exchanges other than specialists to do at least 80 percent of their buying and selling as agents for customers they did not control. Though the rule was revoked in 1976 before it could take effect, the prospect was enough to freeze movement toward institutional membership on the exchanges while the 1975 amendments to the securities acts were being debated.

Both the Carter SEC under Williams and the Reagan SEC under Shad assumed that the problems the staff and the commission addressed themselves to in the early 1970s had been cured by the elmination of fixed commissions. But regulatory arbitrage is not just a matter of the net prices that can be charged under different regulatory regimes; it is the whole complex of ways to make more money under one set of regulations than under another. The shift from Bill Casey's SEC to John Shad's (and, one fears, Richard Breeden's) is a shift from the attitude that the protection of the public might require stiffening the regs of the more permissive market, to the attitude that the preservation of liquidity in the less easy-going market might require a loosening of the regulations there, even if the public might as a result become more endangered.

The commission has even declined to move on situations documented by the House Government Operations Committee, wherein brokers in effect have borrowed customers' stock to lend to short sellers without the customers' knowledge, creating what staff director Don Tucker of that committee calls "a fractional reserve system in securities." Because both lenders to short sellers and purchasers from them believe they own the stock, there are more shares "owned" than are registered with the company; the possibility exists that more proxies will be voted than there are shares. Richard Ketchum, director of the SEC Division of Market Regulation, pooh-poohed the concern at congressional hearings, because "short selling contributes to general pricing efficiency of the equities markets"—and, anyway, not many people vote their proxies.[10]

Instead of leaning on the British to police trading in U.S. securities in London, the SEC approved a proposed NYSE trading session for programs from which the prices of individual stocks could not be reported or deduced. (Floyd Norris of *The New York Times*, who had come to *The Times* from *Barron's* and was relatively sympathetic to the industry, headlined his Sunday piece "The S.E.C. and the Death of Disclosure."[11]) At a Federal Reserve Board symposium in Washington in 1989, the SEC's Ketchum told a group of bankers and bank regulators that speeding up the clearing and settlement of trades was a top priority for the SEC, because the faster trades settled the sooner the brokerage houses that supplied most of the liquidity to the market by trading for their own account would get their money back and could reenter the game. Though he looked at the lectern before him quite earnestly throughout his talk, he and the SEC press department later said the talk had been given without a written text and there was nothing that could be given to a journalist who wished to quote it accurately.

To take one of many examples of the change at the agency from policeman to advocate: Bill Casey's SEC had been deeply troubled about the give-up phenomenon, the direction of brokerage commission business by bank trust departments to brokers who kept large balances in the bank; by mutual funds to brokers who sold a lot of shares in the funds; by state and municipal pension funds to brokers who contributed appropriately to the right political parties; by union-trusteed pension funds to brokers who would kick back to appropriate people in the union leadership. Concern over pension fund assets led Congress in 1974 to include in the Employee Retirement Income Security Act (ERISA) a provision forbidding pension funds to pay brokers more than would be necessary to accomplish the execution of their trades.

The uproar this provision provoked in the brokerage community was so great that the next year, passing the 1975 Securities and Exchange Act amendments, Congress gave pension funds a "safe harbor" in Section 28e-1, which is I think peculiar enough in its phraseology to be worth a quote:

> No person . . . shall be deemed to have acted unlawfully or to have breached a fiduciary duty under State or Federal law unless expressly provided to the contrary by a law enacted by the Congress or any State subsequent to the date of enactment of the Securities Acts Amendments in 1975 solely by reason of his having caused the account to pay a member of an exchange, broker, or dealer an amount of commission for effecting a securities transaction in excess of the amount of commission another member of an exchange, broker or dealer would have charged for effecting that transaction, if such persons determined in good faith that such amount of commission was reasonable in relation to the value of the particular transaction or his overall responsibilities with respect to the accounts as to which he exercises investment discretion.

The "good faith" requirement bugged the lawyers for the securities firms, however, and research on Wall Street fell on hard times. Then Shad took over the SEC and let it be known that the commission would not second-guess decisions by fund managers to pay brokers more than might be necessary. Wall Street entered the era of the "soft dollar," directed shares of commission payments that the broker executing the purchases or sales would pay to someone who provided other services to the customer. In Shad's last year as chairman, 1986, the commission officially broadened its definitions of the research services that could be bought with soft dollars. Business picked up in Gstaad and on the Riviera, in Vail and Maui.

ERISA had given the Department of Labor concurrent jurisdiction over the conduct of pension fund investing, and by an odd circumstance the assistant secretary who came to be in charge of that area in 1982 was Robert G. Monks, a maverick who owed nothing to any politician and would not need a job from anyone when he left. A quizzical, soft-spoken tall man with a mop of hair and a squint, Monks was a descendant of the Vanderbilt family. (It was Monks who hung on Mike Milken, before he copped his plea, the ultimate descriptor: "The candy man.") He had been the largest shareholder in and CEO of The Boston Company, a trust company located as the name indicates. When he sold his bank to what was then called Shearson Hayden Stone (in turn about to be acquired by American Express), he looked around for something useful to do. Having run a trust company, he thought he had some expertise in supervising the probity of pension fund management, and for a wonder the White House agreed.

Eventually, Monks left the Labor Department to found a lobbying and pressure group called Institutional Shareholders Services, which got to be well known in 1991 when he stood for election to the Sears Roebuck board and roused a number of institutions to support him. Before departing, Monks recruited an SEC supervisor named Charles Lerner to come to Labor and head up its section on ERISA supervision. Lerner became a gadfly to the SEC, commissioning studies by Berkowitz and Logue, among others, on the costs of institutional trading. Among the discoveries in these studies was the interesting fact that while mutual funds as a group performed just a little better than the various averages, pension funds consistently performed worse. Lerner also became a nag on the subject of soft dollars. On July 24, 1989, prodded into action by Lerner, the SEC held a Round Table on soft dollars, and decided, hell, it wasn't so bad. Probably enhanced liquidity.

The fact that the Labor Department was in the game led some Wall Street houses that felt themselves victimized by soft-dollar artists to take their complaints to a new address. To general amazement, Goldman Sachs & Co. and Morgan Stanley Group Inc. on February 26, 1990 sent a long "white paper" on soft dollars to then Secretary of Labor Elizabeth Dole. "Soft dollar-related trades," these experts reported, "account for an estimated 20 to 25 percent of broker-dealer firms' listed commissions, and possibly as much as 30 to 50 percent of total trades on the New York Stock Exchange." The charge in brief was that pension "plan assets are being diverted from being used for the exclusive benefit of plan participants and beneficiaries, and instead are being used for the benefit of other clients of the manager or the manager himself." The situation was so bad, Goldman and Morgan argued, that "soft dollar activity threatens the security of employees' retirement income."[12]

Worse still, Morgan and Goldman argued, soft-dollar arrangements stole business from firms like themselves, which could do better executions for the institutions, and gave it to firms less competent to handle trading but prepared to give up more of their commission revenue to buy other services for the funds managers. This, they said, touching what they knew to be the SEC's hot button, reduced the effective liquidity of the market, because "traditional" brokers that offered research services as part of what the customer got for his commissions were much more likely to do block positioning, an activity at which "broker/dealers generally lose money."[13] (That claim touched a different hot button at Rochdale Securities, an investment advisory-cum-brokerage house which receives fees for its RSCO$T service through soft dollars; Rochdale noted that by demanding the right to profitable executions to offset the cost of positioning in other transactions, the large firms were admitting that one account might be providing "a subsidy for the benefit of another account.")[14]

Neglected by the SEC, the soft-dollar phenomenon spread and infected the underwriting system—the system that raises new money for business (which the stock market, as noted, does not). Even at their most generous, commissions on institutional trades in the stock market were rarely as much as one-quarter of 1 percent of the total purchase or sale price of the securities traded. But commissions on Initial Public Offerings (IPOs; when companies "go public") might run as much as 5 percent and were commonly 3 percent. Such securities had not historically commanded the attention of pension funds, which had been encouraged by the "prudent man rule" to invest in seasoned securities. In 1991, however, the institutions grabbed for new equity—an unusually high fraction of which, incidentally, thereupon ran into downdrafts in what was otherwise an up market. Several knowledgeable observers noted that the popularity of IPOs, and of ·equity offerings in general, had arisen in large part because they enabled fund managers to allocate underwriting markup dollars as well as commissions. It may also be worthy of note that the first attempt in years to run around the underwriters by selling significant quantities of bargain-priced "rights" to existing shareholders (a Time-Warner effort that had other problems, too) was gunned down by a barrage of institutional sales.

Closing the Disclosure Gate

In early 1990, the rot that had been spreading at the SEC reached the heart of the agency's function: the disclosure of the terms and conditions of paper to be sold to the public, and of the operations of the company issuing the paper. As part of the Securities Act of 1933, the rules for such disclosure had preceded the organization of the commission, and tampering with them was an act that could have grave consequences. Indirectly, moreover, such tampering made a statement of the commission's attitudes that would affect behavior throughout the markets.

Speaking in fall 1990 to Soviet authorities planning to open a securities market in their country, securities lawyer George R. Krouse, Jr., told his hosts that "The single most destructive element to a fair marketplace is that some participants engage on the basis of information not shared by all. The U.S. securities laws are designed to provide everyone with the fullest information about the marketplace."[15] With the adoption of Rule 144a in April 1990, after almost two years of debate, the deregulation-minded SEC, having erroneously acquiesced to initiatives by others that reduced the transparency of the markets, deliberately, on its own motion, introduced such destruction to the American securities markets.

The vehicle chosen was expansion of "private placement" activity. From the beginning, the commission had given companies an exemption from registration and disclosure requirements if the securities issue involved was in essence either the sale of part of the company to an investor or a borrowing from a large lender that happened to be expressed as bonds rather than as a loan. The rule of thumb was that such paper could be sold without SEC registration to no more than fifty investors who were thereafter forbidden to sell it to anyone outside the group for at least three years. The advantage to the issuer was that he escaped the costs of registration and of public issuance (underwriters handling private placements imposed no sales charges and smaller fees; sometimes such placements could be done without underwriters). The advantage to the purchaser was that in return for sacrificing liquidity he could get a better interest rate or valuable rights to convert debt paper or preferred stock to common equity at a good price.

In the 1960s, the heyday of private placement in the equity market, purchasers of what was called "letter stock" often had a further advantage. Because there was no market for much of this stuff, they could put whatever price they wished on it in reporting to their shareholders or plan sponsors on the success of their investments. (This was also part of the attraction of junk bond purchases in the 1980s.) When the stock market headed south in 1969, a number of "hedge funds" and cheapjack insurance companies were revealed to have misvalued their portfolios of private placement paper (presaging again what would happen with junk bonds twenty years later).

Rule 144a was the brainchild of Linda Quinn, director of the SEC's Division of Corporation Finance. As described by S. L. Mintz in one of the earliest articles on the subject, it "would allow institutional investors to freely trade most privately placed securities among themselves. That would make private placements as liquid as many public debt offerings, but without the hassle and expense of SEC registration." Institutions with more than $100 million in assets would qualify for participation in this market. Trading in 144a issues would not have to be reported to anybody in any way, except to the extent that the annual reports of the companies that bought and sold the paper would reveal their activity in this market. What with the elimination of the costs of registration statements (and the legal liability for misstatements), and the opportunity to trade the stuff back and forth among friends without anybody knowing what you were doing, Rule 144a could really open up the markets. Mintz quoted Linda Quinn: "'Nothing in securities law now would assure that the private placement market doesn't become the primary source of capital.'"[16]

The rationale for 144a was simply stated in the original SEC commentary when the new rule was put out for comment: "The key . . . is that certain institutions can fend for themselves and that, therefore, offers and sales to such institutions do not involve a public offering." Liquidity again: Because they could sell the paper, institutions would be more willing to buy it. And globalization again: One of the reasons foreign corporations did not use the American market as a place to raise capital was the extent of the disclosure our laws required before paper could be sold to the public. Under 144a, a company would not have to disclose more to sell stock in the United States than it would have to disclose in the country of its incorporation—Lichtenstein, for example. In January 1989, the SEC held a public hearing on the proposed Rule 144a, and *sixteen hundred* people came. Among the questions was how to define the institutions that would not need protection in the form of disclosure rules. Someone from Salomon Brothers, a house much more closely involved in trading than in corporate issuance, observed sourly that most of those S&Ls that were in process of costing the taxpayer some hundreds of billions of dollars would qualify for exemption under Rule 144a. Then SEC chairman David Ruder confessed he had not thought about that before, and the project was taken back in house for further study.

As I had occasion to tell SEC commissioner Joseph Grundfest at the time, what was bothering Salomon was the commission's failure to understand the unspoken "unless" clause. Traders in the new market for Rule 144a securities would not have to report their trades *unless they wanted to.* To the extent that Rule 144a securities were easily substitutable for securities traded in public, institutions could whipsaw broker/dealers. And the ganefs who were running so many of the S&Ls would do just that, perhaps with a little help from friends like Mike Milken, who was still up and around and conceding nothing.

Worse: At the heart of the reasoning that led to Rule 144a was a fallacy contradicted by the Investment Company Act, by ERISA, and by the shared experience of nonacademic and nonlegal mankind. Rule 144a—passed, it should be noted, two months after Goldman and Morgan warned the Department of Labor that soft-dollar arrangements were funneling money from pension funds to their managers to such an extent that the funds were endangered—assumed that the interests of the people who managed money for pension funds and mutual funds were identical to the interests of the beneficiaries of the funds. It assumed, too, that these managers had the ability to hunt up and judge the information that would no longer be handed to them on a silver platter in registration statements.

The SEC, commissioners and staff alike, also assumed—against all the evidence from the foreign exchange and municipal bond markets—that the holders of Rule 144a securities, because they would want to trade the paper, would have to publicize their transactions. The NASD, the SEC staff said, would open a special electronic service to facilitate such trading. As indeed, later, it did—a service called Portal, with clearing and settlement done abroad, away from SEC supervision, at CEDEL in Luxembourg. Almost nobody used it (six months after Portal opened, there were only two issues being traded on the system), because people who don't have to trade in public won't trade in public. When Portal failed to draw any business, the American Stock Exchange, Reuters, and the Depository Trust Corporation all suggested Rule 144a market services that would not publicize prices or leave an audit trail, and NASD asked for similar courtesies. As of this writing, the SEC has not summoned the guts to give this store away, too.

Early in 1990, David Ruder resigned as chairman of the SEC and Richard Breeden, who had chaired Vice President George Bush's task force on financial services during the Reagan days, succeeded him. Breeden professed himself concerned about the sacrifice of transparency involved in Rule 144a (though he noted quite properly that other markets were even less transparent), and put a few more qualifications into the rule. Institutions to trade in this market would have to show not only $100 million in assets but also at least $25 million in net worth (thus excluding most of the S&L cowboys). In addition, the securities issued and traded could not be interchangeable with securities already issued and traded in the public markets. In an interview in early 1991, Breeden said that meant no letter stock, no equity, which came as news to several companies that *had* issued equity under Rule 144a, and an SEC spokesperson clarified Breeden's meaning: All he *really* said was that all paper including stock issued under Rule 144a would have to be significantly different from other issues of that company's paper traded in the market. That ruled out straight equity? Well, maybe not; there could be ways to differentiate.

Europeans, in any event, thought Rule 144a was intended as an invitation to sell stock to American investors without going through the former colonials' odd disclosure rituals. Deborah Hargreaves expressed surprise in *The Financial Times* that "although the attractions of issuing equity under the new rules were expected to be greater than those for debt, in fact the market for debt and convertible securities has taken off more quickly than that for straight equity."[17] In fact, nothing took off very far or very high, mostly because in the climate of 1990 American buyers wanted the kind of information they got in the traditional SEC registration statement, not the personal assurances and unaudited assertions commonplace in the selling of European issues.

Rule 144a had missed its market. Real estate limited partnerships, documented about as well as Rule 144a prospectuses, were failing all over the country, costing investors (most of whom had found out about this kind of investing from their stockbrokers) not only the money they lost because the real estate wasn't worth what the partnership had paid for it but also the tax deductions on these properties they had already taken in previous years. The institutions supposedly eager for such paper were struggling with what were turning out to be inadequate covenants on junk bonds. Worse, their pieces of loans made by money-center banks—in a "loan participation market" very similar to what the SEC projected for Rule 144a bonds—were turning sour in alarming ways. Investors no longer felt that they could safely avoid the costs of "due diligence" on loans where they did not have the protection of securities act disclosure. And if they *were* going to buy these pigs in a poke that the SEC had designed for them, they sure as hell wanted a premium in the rates they were paid. The premium for inadequate documentation wound up in many cases larger than the premium for illiquidity that Linda Quinn thought she was eliminating.

Still, the rule is now in place. Coupled with the permission to the New York Stock Exchange to run opaque after-hours trading sessions and a proposal to excuse foreign issuers from any American disclosure requirements greater than those in their home country provided Americans hold less than 10 percent of the stock, it signals a retreat from what has always been the central American principle of regulation. This sort of retreat inevitably becomes a rout. As James D. Cox, a law professor at Duke University, told *The New York Times,* "These developments ultimately will mean the watering down of the domestic requirements. You can't live long in as politically attuned an environment as the S.E.C. and impose lighter requirements on a company from Japan than one from Peoria."[18]

"To me," wrote Commissioner Edward H. Fleischman, dissenting from the decision to approve the NYSE crossing session for anonymous programs, "the primary reason to promote the return to domestic markets of trades in domestic stocks currently being executed overseas is to reveal them to the marketplace so that their significance may be known and assessed by other market participants. . . . The American securities markets, in my view, do and will compete with foreign markets for trades on the basis of the unrivalled fundamental strengths of the American markets: liquidity, transparency, ease of entry, and breadth of participation. To sacrifice one of these strengths—transparency—and thereby to diminish the others is for me too high a price to pay to accomplish the laudable purpose of furthering the domestic markets' role in international market competition."[19] But he stood alone. In October 1991, he had another occasion for a solitary dissent, when the SEC, shockingly, approved an NASD application for an early-morning trading session that would permit American dealers in American stocks to withhold information on their purchases and sales.

James Robertson, an ex-FBI agent who had become vice-chairman of the Federal Reserve Board, once described this game, then played among the federal and state banking regulators, as a "competition in laxity." The ultimate cost to the taxpayer in S&L and bank failures in the last dozen years of this century will be greater than the total expenditure of the federal government on elementary and secondary education during that period. The United States cannot win such a game against the Japanese or the Europeans (who are trying to "harmonize" their own securities regulations in a way that will allow them to poach other people's business), let alone the residents of the Netherlands Antilles, Lichtenstein, and the Channel Islands. American markets have been the world's strongest through years when American savings rates did not justify it because they were the most transparent and the most trustworthy. SEC Chairman Breeden seems prepared to give that away for a mess of pottage. As Floyd Norris wrote in *The Times,* "American standards of financial disclosure could wither away. If Mr. Breeden is not careful, that may end up being the legacy of his term as S.E.C. chairman."

Nickels and Dimes

The regulators who chose the wrong path could make a theoretical case for what they did. Shad was not entirely wrong on the unfairness of holding the chief executives of giant companies personally responsible for the defalcations of their underlings. But fiduciary relationships are by definition unfair to the fiduciary: "A trustee," Judge Benjamin Cardozo wrote in a famous opinion while still on the New York State Court of Appeals, "is held to something stricter than the morals of the market place. Not honesty alone, but the punctilio of an honor the most sensitive, is the standard of behavior. . . . Uncompromising rigidity has been the attitude of courts of equity when petitioned to undermine the rule of undivided loyalty by the 'disintegrating erosion' of particular exceptions. Only thus has the level of conduct for fiduciaries been kept at a level higher than that trodden by the crowd."[20] That sort of thing costs money, and doubtless impedes efficiency. There were reasons, however, which Shad as a lawyer should have understood, why society has thought such prices should be paid—and, incidentally, why people honored as fiduciaries have been willing to pay them. Respect is also a coin in a well-managed realm.

The decision to let specialists elect the participation of percentage orders on a more liberal basis was not without justification in terms of a public policy that wishes to see the knowledge of as many trades as possible disseminated to the entire investing public. As the Milbank Tweed brief argued, Congress in 1934 or even 1975 had no view on how the market should address "the 'large agency order'—an order that, because its very size affects its market, cannot be executed in the fashion of a conventional market or limit order for only a few hundred shares."[21] One could argue, as the Stock Exchange did in its original request, that the very small danger of manipulation when a closely watched specialist activated orders for his own convenience should be set against the much greater danger to public investors when block positioners and institutional fund managers worked hand in glove to cross trades, allegedly in London, after the close of the U.S. markets.

Whatever its validity, however, this was not an argument the SEC *could* accept. "The black-letter law" is the only reason the

SEC (or any other regulatory agency) has authority over anything or anybody. As long as there is reason to believe that a regulatory change that contradicts the agency's legal mandate does in fact risk the damage Congress wished to guard against, the agency has no option but to go to Congress if it wishes to permit what the law forbids.

Soft dollars are not a vice in themselves (though a trader who first went to work in the market during the 1960s insists that current arrangements are inherently more deceptive than the give-ups in the age of fixed commissions because the give-ups were an open and aboveboard allocation of funds that left an audit trail). And it is a new definition of chutzpah for Morgan Stanley to complain that the soft-dollar boutiques are depriving it of the order flow it requires to give the market liquidity at difficult moments. The commissioners' argument, however, rests on their clearly false belief that the plan sponsors—the corporations that set up the pension funds—know what the managers of their investments are doing in the allocation of brokerage commissions. The notion that the fund managers and the plan sponsors have an identity of interest is a product of academic fantasy reinforced by reluctance to regulate. Soft-dollar payments could be defended if they were a matter of public record. But the Bush administration in its heart thinks there is already too much public disclosure, of everything.

Even Rule 144a, considered out of context, has a background that gives it a degree of plausibility. Forbidden to underwrite securities by the Glass-Steagall Act of 1933, and disintermediated from their traditional role as short-term lenders by a commercial paper market controlled by the brokerage houses, money-center banks in the 1980s developed a system of loan participations by which the originators could sell pieces of their loans just as if they were bonds. Loan participations were traded much as bonds were traded at trading desks that sat cheek by jowl with the bond trading desks, by the same insurance companies, pension funds, and bank trust departments that traded bonds. In 1990, one of the most rapidly growing categories of mutual funds was the so-called "prime-rate fund" that bought pieces of bank loans. Public disclosure of bank loans was a null class; as Lowell Bryan of McKinsey & Co. wrote, banks could not live without deposit insurance because people who put their money in a bank were in effect financing a "blind pool" of assets. Innocent insurance companies and pension funds and small banks buying these loan participations were not even protected by NASD rules against gouging by dealers. At least there would be some public announcement of the issuance, if not the trading, of Rule 144a securities.

The reason people want opacity, as the authors of the Securities Acts knew and modern professors of finance have never learned, is that it's easier to make money if nobody can see what you're doing. Ken McLean, while staff director of the Senate Banking Committee, said in 1988 with reference to proprietary trading, "We always assume that these guys up there are cheating the public for nickels and dimes." But it never stays nickels and dimes: In markets as elsewhere, the appetite grows with eating. As the participants in these markets seek to maximize their return, they can find plenty of allies in the press and the universities to explain incomprehensibly that honesty and openness are too costly to be preserved in an age when information is incredibly plenteous and unimaginably cheap. Since 1981 the dominant school of thought in the SEC, and indeed in the executive branch, has held that unless a profitable activity is actually, specifically, unarguably illegal, the government should simply roll over and enjoy it.

The government has been ineffective or worse in combating the deterioration of our markets mostly because, since the early 1970s, nobody has paid much attention to why so much has gone wrong. The technology exists to give us markets *more* transparent, more honest, more effective as guides to the allocation of resources. We and our children and our trading partners will live better if we can achieve such markets, but first we have to want them and then we have to figure out how we can get them.

"If we could first know where we are, and whither we are tending," Abraham Lincoln said, "we could better judge what to do, and do it better." In the securities markets, too.

CHAPTER 8

Remote and Opaque

The diminution of our markets as major factors in the allocation of resources began with the gargantuan growth of corporate pension funds. These funds were born mostly in the period between 1941 and 1953, or World War II and the end of the Korean War, when corporate tax rates were over 50 percent, personal income taxes acquired a superbracket of 92 percent, and money allocated to employee pensions could be deducted from income for tax purposes. As an employee of Dell Publishing Co. said when Albert Delacorte decided to start a pension plan, "The old bastard finally found somebody he hated more than he hates the people who work for him." The trade unions and their members came to understand that a dollar of wages would be taxed (as would the earnings on any dollar of savings), whereas a dollar contributed by an employer to a pension plan would go into the pension fund without tax, and would earn and keep earning, compounded, without tax on the earnings.

Pension plans, like life insurance companies that stick to their last, are exponential growers, because the payments that come in are always greater than the benefits that go out. The money that poured into these funds began to be invested in large chunks through markets designed to process small orders from individuals. Not surprisingly, the existing market process misfired.

The visible problem in the 1960s was the commission system, with its rigid price per 100 shares. The industry defended this system (people will defend any law or custom that makes money for them) by the argument that high commissions were required as risk insurance for the "block positioners," the broker/dealer firms who took the other side of some ponderable proportion of large institutional transactions to help institutional buyers and sellers (especially sellers) conduct their business. If these brokers-turned-dealers didn't have the cushion of high commissions on the entire trade to compensate them for the losses they might suffer when disposing of the dregs of their positions, they would be out of the game and institutions would cease to buy common stocks because they'd have no way to get out of their investments.

The passage of time saw continuous rapid growth of institutional trading—block trading, defined as transactions involving more than 10,000 shares—from an average of 9 trades a day in 1965 to 136 per day in 1975 (the year fixed commissions ended), 528 per day in 1980, and 3,693 per day (the record) in 1987. The proportion of New York Stock Exchange trading represented by these large orders was 3.1 percent in 1965, peaking at 54.5 percent in 1988. Total annual trading on the NYSE, meanwhile, went from a range of 13 to 28 percent of all shares listed on the exchange in the 1960s and 1970s to 73 percent of listed shares in 1987.[1] These numbers do not include the trading on the regional exchanges, or in London, or on The Crossing Network.

Some of these numbers are a little misleading. Of the ten largest block transactions in the history of the exchange, six came in 1988, and all six were pairs of transactions of the same or almost the same size (one pair took 26 *million* shares of Occidental Petroleum, switched them to new hands briefly, and then restored them to the original holder), with the turnaround accomplished during the course of a single trading day. Most of these trades were done for Japanese insurance companies that could take dividends without paying taxes on them, and could take a tax loss from the drop in the price of the stock "ex-dividend," on the day after the day when stockholders of record were entitled to the dividend. Commissions paid to brokers on such business were all but invisible; they obliged as an accommodation to customers who were sources of much other business.

The reported rash of trading was also for real, however: Pension funds, mutual funds, insurance companies, and the common funds of bank trust departments were buying and selling on the public market in quantities far beyond the absorptive capacity of the normal flow of orders from dentists in Chicago and realtors in Los Angeles. The normal operations of the exchange floor were no longer the basic source of transactions. ("The only time institutional personnel concern themselves with limit orders," Laszlo Birinyi, Jr., wrote in his booklet for newcomers to Salomon, "is during the registered representative exam. Limit orders—as defined by textbooks, brokers, training, and NYSE publicity blurbs—are unknown in the real world."[2]) Brokers who handled institutional business now were charged with finding through their own information resources buyers for sellers and sellers for buyers on individual large orders for individual stocks— and it was increasingly part of their service to pick up as traders for their own account some part of the deal they brokered.

As the authors of the Securities and Exchange Act of 1934 understood from their own recent and bitter experience, this way of doing business put the broker/dealer firms in a conflict of interest. Representing the pension fund that wished to buy shares of Westinghouse, they were obligated as agents to find the lowest price, but as the traders who would wind up selling the stock short for a while to fill the Westinghouse order, they wanted a block price high enough so it would go down after the institution's purchase was finished. Because the SEC was playing Cheshire Cat, because finance economics saw each trade as an atomized and complete transaction—and because lawyers didn't care one way or another so long as their clients made the money to pay their fees—there was nobody to point out that this way of doing business was a primrose path.

Salaries and commissions in the high hundreds of thousands began to be paid to the "institutional salesmen" who found the customers that took the broker/dealer firms out of the positions they assumed to sell the blocks. One notes the change in occupational title from "representative" or "customer's man" to "salesman." Those who serviced or otherwise profited from the institutional accounts became, to quote the title the publisher put on a book of mine in 1968, the *New Breed on Wall Street*. They were smarter than most of their predecessors, and also often (the hedge fund operator Mike Steinhardt, who was one of them, said the other day that he looked through my book once in a while to see who was still out of jail) less trustworthy.

Inevitably, the weight of public concern over these changes was for the holders of the mutual fund shares and the beneficiaries of the pension plans and insurance policies. Institutions, after all, were not giant investment banks: They were surrogates for little people. At the same time, however, policy-makers were concerned that decisions made by a handful of money managers working for very large funds would push prices around regardless of economic logic. In the early 1970s, after the speculative fever of the late 1960s had left everybody exhausted, the people who managed large funds spoke of "one-decision" stocks that you bought and put away forever; outsiders spoke of a "nifty fifty." A market researcher once said that the initials IBM stood for "If I buy their equipment I can't be fired for it." Similarly, money managers would buy IBM and the rest of the companies that had the largest market capitalization, because they could not be criticized for doing so.

There was an element of avoidance here. By purchasing and holding the high-capitalization stocks, the institutions made the fewest waves in the market. They defused any objections to their market role by accepting a status as price-takers rather than price-setters. A growing body of empirically based theory proclaimed that nobody could "beat the market." Because all the currently available information about a stock was already imbedded in its price, money managers would do as well throwing darts at a stock table as they could running all the advice they received through the most sophisticated computer programs. (Remember Leibniz: the best of all possible worlds. John Maynard Keynes, Peter Lynch of Magellan Fund, Benjamin Graham and his friend David Dodd and their protegé Warren Buffett had all beaten the market consistently, but every probability distribution has to allow for occasional freak results.) There was some question about what information was really important. Burton G. Malkiel, publicist of the "random walk" theory of the stock market, noted in a study with John Cragg that if you could know the predictions of stock analysts a year from now you would be able to predict prices better than if you just knew how well the company would do in the next twelve months.[3] The theory served nicely to explain the investment results of pension funds, insurance companies, and bank trust departments, which on average produced returns for their beneficiaries that trailed the changes in the stock averages and indexes. The averages and indexes, after all, do not deduct management or trading costs.

As the funds grew larger, the theoreticians of these subjects increasingly recommended that they be "passive investors." The ultimate of passive investing is the "index fund," which buys all the stocks in the S&P 500—a nifty fifty writ large. Providentially, the development of the futures and options markets in Chicago gave the money managers access to riskless intermarket trading activities that could enhance their return from passive investing.

The legal situation for these funds was somewhat unclear. Over the years, the courts had developed a "prudent man rule" for fiduciaries, limiting a money manager's investment of other people's money to categories of supposedly very safe instruments. State and municipal pension funds were often restricted to municipal and federal bonds, which was especially silly because the pension funds paid no taxes on their earnings, municipal bonds paid lower interest than other bonds because their payments were tax-exempt, and federal bonds paid lower interest than corporate bonds in part because the interest paid on them was exempt from state and municipal tax. As inflation crept up on the country, moreover, it began to be recognized that simply funding the pensions that would have to be paid at today's wage scales would not be adequate protection for future pensioners, who would be living in a world of much higher prices by the time they retired. Common stocks have historically been a hedge against inflation. One could argue convincingly that no prudent man would invest all his retirement moneys in fixed-income instruments. Most pension funds had always invested some fraction of their money in stocks; now they were encouraged to increase the fraction. ERISA preempted the common-law definitions of prudence and gave the money managers much greater freedom.

For some time after the passage of ERISA, however, there was a substantial school of thought that institutional investors should not trade in and out of the market. First, they couldn't: Orders in sizes meaningful to them would swamp the market and move the prices. Second, churning these huge accounts would generate huge commission costs to the fund. Third, they were in theory the repository of high time horizons in American decision making: Because they had long-term liabilities, they should take a long-term view in their acquisition of assets. Nifty fifty and passive investing strategies were thus seen as inevitable regardless of efficient market theories. Because they couldn't trade in and out without pushing the prices in directions adverse to their interests, institutions would be less willing to hold stocks than to hold, say, government bonds. They would demand a premium in yield to compensate them for the loss of liquidity.

By extension of this argument, it was clear that if the markets found a way to improve the liquidity of large blocks of stock, institutions would be more willing to hold stock, and it was sound public policy to encourage institutions to hold stock. Institutional ownership would be good for the markets because it would increase demand for stocks and would be good for industry because it would make equity more salable. It would be good for the quality of management, the SEC advised, because "the collectivization of otherwise disparate shareholder interests through institutional investment has created the most formidable counter-force to corporate managerial hegemony."[4] The higher the proportion of equity on the balance sheet, the more stable the company.

One notes in passing that these theories did not work. Institutional shareholders left relations with the companies in their portfolios to their money managers, who were interested in nothing but the performance of the stock. For them, the Wall Street rule—if you don't like the management, sell the stock—had always been more important than the prudent man rule; they had no interest in influencing corporate governance. This attitude changed only in the late 1980s, when public companies began to adopt "poison pills" that made it much harder for take-over artists to grab them. As the prospect for take-over or buy-out was a source of premium prices for stocks, money managers looking to cash out before the quarterly statements of their achievements went to their masters began to take an interest in what the boards of corporations did. It is by no means clear that money managers *should* take that much of an interest in corporate governance: George McNamee of the old-line brokerage house First Albany scoffs that "We ask speculators masquerading as pension funds who should be running the big companies."

Institutional ownership did not by any means increase the proportion of equity in corporate capital. The years of escalating institutional ownership were years of unprecedented—unimaginable—improvement in the liquidity of large blocks of stock, and they were also a time when corporations redeemed their stock in unprecedented—unimaginable—quantities, leaving corporate balance sheets at the end of a decade of prosperity more distressed than they had been in the past after years of recession. Ignoring stock splits, the number of shares in the companies traded on the New York Stock Exchange declined by eight *billion* between 1981 and 1990.

Moreover, the system has become spectacularly expensive by comparison with its contribution to the real economy. Professor Louis Lowenstein of Columbia Law School has noted that in 1986 the broker/dealer community took in revenues of $32 billion while raising only that same $32 billion in new equity investment for enterprise.[5] Despite the great growth of contract thrifts like pension funds and life insurers, the nation's total savings in the 1980s were negative—we had to import foreign capital to finance our government deficits and investment needs.

What does a large institution want from its brokers? The same thing an individual customer wants—advice and order execution. What is especially valued is "the first call." It is practically impossible for a broker to put out a recommendation simultaneously to every one of its customers. The customer who gets the recommendation first buys at a lower price or sells at a higher price than others. If it's a big enough house making the recommendation, and a strong enough story, the customer doesn't even have to worry about whether the case for buying the stock is valid: Enough sheep will follow that there will be money in leading the flock. Some of the give-ups in today's market-place direct money from the brokers who execute the trades to boutique shops that circle around the institutions to pass information from one to another, bees visiting the flowers. Whether one wishes to describe the first call as research or not is a matter of taste. If the authors of the "research" have taken a large position for themselves (or—worse—are engaged in selling out their positions), another word would doubtless be more suitable. But the first call is unquestionably the most valued output of securities "research."

In the 1960s and early 1970s, institutions earned the first call by the volume of their business, commissions being fixed. Today, says Harry Keefe, who left his own long-established firm of Keefe Bruyette & Wood to operate a fund that specializes in bank stock investments (and short sales), you can get the first call by paying higher commissions—and you get the last call when you pay lower commissions. "The City of New York pension funds boasted the other day that for years they've never paid more than three cents a share commissions," Keefe said recently. "When I was a broker, why did I call somebody who wouldn't pay me more than three cents a share? Because I wanted to get rid of something; there couldn't be any other reason." One can make a plausible case that pension funds do much less well than mutual funds in the market because the pension funds feel constrained to pay the lowest commissions, while the mutual funds are prepared to pay for the services they buy.

When the SEC decided to go to fully negotiable commissions, Gus Levy of Goldman Sachs warned the commissioners and the institutions that they were going to turn an agency relationship into an adversarial relationship. ERISA then set the terms of the war by stressing the obligation of money managers to negotiate low prices for the services brokers performed for institutional investors. The institutions have a point in their insistence that they did not drive down the commissions the brokers charged them—it was competition among the brokers themselves that sent commissions tumbling by three-quarters and more. But once transactions were being executed for one pension fund at prices of two and three cents a share, others felt compelled to seek the same bargains. In addition, the willingness of brokers to split off soft dollars from commissions as low as three cents a share argues that the order flow was valuable even at those prices.

What made the order flow valuable, however, was not the commission itself but the information, which could be used in the firm's proprietary trading or "sold" (not for anything so vulgar as cash) to others in the market. I. W. ("Tubby") Burnham, chairman of Drexel Burnham and former chairman of the Securities Industries Association, wrote a letter to *The Wall Street Journal* pointing out (as part of his opposition to a proposed transaction tax) that "Those who really handle the large amounts of institutional money have the discretion to buy and sell whenever they wish and increase the volatility on both sides."[6] Once the Chicago markets were up and flying, the broker/dealers could exploit intraday volatility (that is, the movement of stock prices between nine-thirty and four) to assure themselves profits on their trading activities. "They ask me at brandy and cigar time," Laszlo Birinyi, Jr., said while still at Salomon Brothers, "'What are we going to do about program trading?' And I say, 'Pay twenty cents a share.'" Frank Weeden shuddered. "Broker/dealer conflicts are like getting tickets fixed. They become acceptable because everybody's doing it. But the weakness of the industry should not be used as a rationalization for doing something wrong."

Slowly, slowly, the institutions began to realize that they were being had. In the 1960s, the institutions had sought to do their trading away from the New York Stock Exchange to avoid the payment of the commissions. In the late 1980s, they began to seek ways to trade away from the exchange so they could conceal their activities from the brokerage houses that were supposed to be their agents.

Submitting to the Congress in 1971 the SEC's report on institutional investors, Commissioner Robert Smith asked in one buried paragraph "a question regarding the degree to which markets used by institutional investors and individual investors could or should be separated."[7] Nobody ever did try to answer that question, and with reason. It's a terribly difficult question. Two different markets for the same things will always be arbitraged. If one of the markets is private and the other is public—the all but inevitable outcome of any plan to separate the institutional and the individual markets—all the money will be made by the participants in the private market. Unconsidered, then, guided by the natural flow of money to profitable use, the separation occurred. Without consideration, the SEC, established to protect the individual investor, encourages the separation. The time is long past when Congress must consider.

Responsibility Abdicated

The problem does not lie in market mechanisms. It lies in the pension funds and the nature of their operations, which are what Hyman Minsky has called "the investment of money twice removed." Such funds now hold almost 40 percent of the equity in American publicly traded corporations, and the responsibilities of their managers do not extend beyond efforts to enrich the fund. Noting similar problems in Britain, *The Financial Times* recently complained that "about a third of the equity capital of British quoted [traded] companies has been channelled into these extraordinarily remote and opaque funds. Not only has this concentration of ownership created a barrier between the broader population and the stock market, but there have been increasing problems of corporate governance because the pension fund managers have failed to accept their full responsibilities of ownership."[8]

Recognition of these responsibilities has been made more difficult by tax laws which reward the issuance of debt and by the discovery early in the 1980s that control of a company is worth more than the pro rata value of the shares when ownership is widely spread. The value of shares is a function of the expected future profits of the company; the value of control is a function of the market price of the assets that can be sold independently of the rest of the company—and a function also of the difference between the discount rate applied to future earnings and the discount rate applied to a promised flow of receipts from debt instruments. By shifting future earnings from future stockholders to future bondholders, the take-over artists may be able to expropriate some portion of those earnings for the benefit of today's stockholders.

If the corporation to be taken over has a well-funded pension plan, the acquirer may be able to take money out of future pensions by closing down the pension plan and buying annuities for present employees. Where Milken the magician was involved, the insurance company (First Executive Life) that sold the annuities would help a Milken client (Charles Hurwitz) buy the company (Pacific Lumber Co.) by purchasing newly issued junk bonds, which would then be used to pay off the annuities the acquirer could buy cheap because First Executive was making such a great return on its assets; and the Milken client could simply pocket that part of the pension plan assets left over after the annuities were purchased. (In fairness, Hurwitz continued the payments to his pensioners when First Executive collapsed.)

The money managers for the institutions loved these deals, which met the need for quarterly profits in the portfolio, and the bias in their favor extended to the heads of the pension plans themselves. Sometimes the situations were far from clear-cut. "I guess I'd have to say our biggest problem was our institutional investors," said Charles Exley of NCR, talking about his effort to fend off a bid from AT&T. "These people were put in a rather strange position. One of them believed that the merger was inevitable and not a good thing. But if you had eight times the investment in AT&T as in NCR, they explained, then you would vote your NCR shares in a manner that would provide the lowest possible price for NCR. The logic is inescapable, but how this all reads on shareholder rights, I'm at a loss to say."[9]

None of it makes any sense at all in terms of the allocation of resources. When T. Boone Pickens was looking to pick up oil companies in the 1980s, the standard statement was that it was cheaper to buy reserves than to explore for and find them. Presumably, the stock market's undervaluation of oil in the ground (which should sell for the marginal cost of finding new oil) was the result of various government controls in the past and the uncertainty as to what controls might be imposed in the future. Don't blame the messenger. But the market operated in the 1980s to leverage government mistakes into large profits for current stockholders, large losses for future stockholders. The eager participation of pension funds and charitable endowments in this swindle measures the loss of *civitas* in America as our economic actors have drawn narrower and narrower boundaries around whatever fiduciary responsibilities they are prepared to acknowledge. Lawyer Saul Cohen cheerfully if obscurely proclaims that "the fiduciary duties of brokers to their customers . . . are ceasing to be recognized by most courts."[10]

Prescription for a Cure

We must now go back to the beginning, and write legislation to give us the markets we need. Despite the large contributions the broker/dealer firms make to selected members of Congress, there would not in fact be major opposition to a thoughtful restructuring. The current structure, though apparently powerful and well supported, is in truth as hollow as an East European state in the last days of Soviet hegemony. In the markets where people now most distrust each other there remains a memory of a time when nobody wanted to be thought of as a pig or a chiseler. Markets are still places where people have to live on close terms with each other, and they would much rather do so without suspicion or rancor. Always and everywhere, it is secrecy that creates mistrust.

The first requirement, then, is renewed commitment by the SEC to the American tradition of transparency. Sunshine is the best disinfectant. Fear that one's actions will be in tomorrow's paper is the best dissuader. Perhaps because the press has mostly done so poor a job in covering these matters, even those apparently most committed to transparency have lost their sense that this dissuasion must be a matter of general public disapproval, not merely a quarrel within the industry. In his admirable dissent from the SEC decision to permit the NYSE to begin its opaque second after-hours trading session, Commissioner Fleischman approved the first crossing session, despite the implied loss of transparency, because if members didn't like it they could stop it: "I believe that the officials and governors of the securities exchanges and the NASD understand their markets more thoroughly than any government regulatory agency (not to speak of any single individual acting in a regulatory role) and will be quick to respond to market reaction labelling their prior initiatives 'wrong.'"[11] But the market reaction will always be more or less neutral—there but for the grace of God—unless there is a public exposure.

There is no reason why the SEC cannot announce that any transfer of the ownership of stock in a U.S. corporation is an American transaction and must be publicly reported in the United States. Such a rule could be enforced through the Depository Trust Corporation. Broker/dealer firms licensed to do business in the United States (a category that includes foreign firms with American subsidiaries) should be forbidden to change the ownership of shares customers have left on their books in "street name" without informing the DTC and printing the transaction at the first opportunity on whatever reporting system is used for the market in which this security trades.

Such a requirement would not represent any greater outreach of U.S. authority than the current Section 8f-2 of the Securities and Exchange Act, which prohibits "any United States person" or "foreign person controlled by a United States person" from borrowing money to carry securities purchases in contravention of Federal Reserve Board regulations. It could not be enforced against foreign firms with no U.S. subsidiary, but one doubts that significant investors in U.S. securities whatever their domicile would wish to run the risk of having their ownership not recognized in the United States.

Reporting requirements on all trades should also be imposed on tax-favored institutional investors, a category that for this purpose should include not only insurance companies but also mutual funds, which are excused from tax on their own profits provided they pay 95 percent of their income through to their shareholders. These requirements should include arrangements to report *immediately,* and should include trades in foreign securities and in commodities, currencies, and options as well as trades of securities subject to SEC registration.

The question of whether public reports should include the identity of the buyer and seller is more complicated. The futures exchanges do require such identification but only for the use of the clearing corporation; the NYSE does not, partly on the argument that a purchaser can operate through so many nominees that the trail peters out before you can use it. (The same argument, however, could be used against the publication of the names of large *holders,* which is already required: Every company must file a form 13-D, listing its largest holders, every quarter.) The public report of who is doing what trading might produce more manipulation than it prevents, though there is again the danger of the unspoken unless clause in today's law: Large traders need not identify themselves *unless* they care to do so. Surely the exchanges as self-regulatory organizations and the SEC should have such information. The identity of the brokers in all trades *and the commissions paid to them* (or the markup taken) should be a matter of public record, although access to the information should probably be restricted. To give the devil his due, one of Richard Breeden's first initiatives as chairman of the SEC was the promotion of a law—which passed—giving the commission authority to require the identification of large traders. And in the summer 1991, the commission announced a rule under which all brokers would be required to assign the same customer number to all large traders, with the record of activity in that account continuously available to the regulators. Testifying in hearings related to Salomon Brothers' jiggery pokery in the government bond auctions, Breeden tentatively suggested that such large-trader reports might be useful in the Treasuries market, too.

Other market reforms, which I have advocated elsewhere, would create friction between the stock index futures markets and the exchange markets, perhaps through a transaction tax, perhaps through restrictions on trading in both markets by the same individual or firm within a certain time period. No public or economic purpose is served by the arbitrage that keeps the stock index and stock markets in lockstep; the specific shares that make up the index should *not* move in lockstep with it, and in the millisecond world of arbitrage there is no time to distinguish the stocks that benefit and the stocks that lose by the news event that triggered the rise or fall of the index. The SEC has already affirmed and made permanent the 1990 NYSE rules which prohibited program purchasing on up-ticks when the market has risen fifty Dow points in a day, or selling on down-ticks when the market has fallen fifty points in a day.

The primary concern, however, must be the behavior of the institutional investors. They should not be speculators; it contradicts their function, which is not simply to "make money" but to agglomerate and employ the savings of the community in ways that will enhance the *future* income of the beneficiaries. There is nothing wrong with speculation. It is a legitimate and useful activity, but it is an ancillary activity, something that should facilitate rather than focus the use of institutional funds. Investment decisions made by pension funds, insurance companies, and charitable endowments are simply too important to the future of the economy and the society to be left floating on the seas of market volatility. Even the mutual funds that act as surrogates for individuals should be discouraged from conducting their business in ways that stress trading rather than investing.

The simplest way to encourage high time horizons in the halls of institutional investors is to tax their profits on short-term trading. To believe that this will reduce the money available to the beneficiaries of these funds is to denigrate the role of investment in the American economy, and also the obvious truth that the real fortunes have been made by picking the right stocks and holding them unless or until some major event makes investment in an industry or company less attractive. Such procedures have been the real security of the upper middle class, always the largest investor in equities. Surely the retirement income of American workers should be a function of the success of the American economy, not of the cleverness of rocket scientists exploiting ten-second "anomalies" in the prices of futures, options, and cash stocks.

The tax exemption given to pension funds and charitable endowments is intended to let the beneficiaries reap all the benefits of compound earnings on their investments, not to make profits on business activities in competition with profit-making enterprise. The classic case is that of New York University and Mueller's Macaroni, which had been left to the university in its entirety by a grateful alumnus. The university declined to pay corporate income tax on the profits of Mueller's, on the grounds that these profits were dedicated to educational uses, and the courts agreed. Congress then passed a law declaring that all profits from profit-seeking businesses were equally taxable, regardless of who owned the business. Trading securities is a business just as making spaghetti is a business, and profit-seeking competitors are disadvantaged trading against tax-exempt entities just as pasta makers would be disadvantaged selling their product against tax-exempt competitors.

Eighty percent of what now ails our securities markets, and some fraction of the misallocation of resources in our economy, could be resolved simply by taxing the funds (including mutual funds) on profits from securities held less than, say, one year. Felix Rohatyn and Warren Buffett (in 1991, surprisingly, CEO of Salomon Brothers, the quintessential trading house) have suggested 100 percent taxation—confiscation of trading profits. That seems unnecessary and unwise, because private speculation is essential to the smooth operation of securities (and commodities) markets. But putting the nonprofit funds and the private traders on a level playing field by making both pay standard corporate profits taxes can do no harm and might do much good.

"Industrial policy" for the United States calls not for the government to assign priorities but for the capital markets to price wisely. As leaders in the capital markets, and beneficiaries of an extraordinary governmental favor, the tax-exempt funds have a special obligation to "pick winners." Ideally, that obligation should be met by capable in-house research departments, especially at the larger funds, but there is no reason why the funds should not look to their brokers for research assistance, and pay them for it when the assistance is provided. These charges should probably be "unbundled," so that economists and analysts who wish to set up in business as advisers to funds are not disadvantaged by having to compete with brokers who can throw in such work as lagniappe with the commission. The symbiosis between execution and research on value would seem to justify carefully policed use of soft dollars to pay for some of this work. One would expect that firms supplying valuable research recommendations would be able to charge higher commissions than firms that just do executions.

If all went well, and the trading floors of the exchanges survived, the separation of the individual and the institutional markets could be accomplished on the floor, as to some extent it is today, by processing all individual orders electronically and requiring institutional orders to work through the auction. Individual orders (up to a thousand shares, less for high-priced stocks) would be automatically executed by specialists or by brokers at the post who had agreed to the assignment to them of public orders, at the existing offer for purchases and the existing bid for sales. (Something of this sort already operates at the Chicago Board Options Exchange, where clerks rip messages off computer printers and slot them into boxes to inform options traders of what has been put into their inventory by the machine.) Institutional orders would go to the floor for participation in the auction, or could at any time be crossed upstairs at the price of the most recent transaction. Toronto's CATS screens, with entry possible from both upstairs offices and the floor, seem a possible starting point for the development of such a trading venue.

This system would leave price discovery largely in the hands of the intermediaries (as it is today), and would maintain the virtues of the single market without giving insiders the opportunity to grab off arbitrage profits. It would probably cost a little more (as it does today) than a system of upstairs screen-based trading. Volume would be lower, especially if transaction taxes increased the cost of what the finance economists now call "noise trading." There would be no reason for spreads to be greater, however, because customers would if anything lose information advantages vis-à-vis the brokers and specialists. Commissions to institutions might or might not be higher: The market would determine, as it now determines, the commissions charged to individuals. There seems to be room for brokers as cheap as Muriel Siebert (who will execute trades for individual customers at rates as low as 3¢ per share) and as expensive as Merrill or Shearson or Prudential or PaineWebber or Dean Witter, all of whom have spent money on advertising to establish brand names that yield them partial monopoly rents. In 1991, the most profitable brokerage firms in proportion to their revenues were Edward D. Jones and A. G. Edwards of St. Louis, both of which gave personal service from chains of what are often one-man offices scattered around the country—and did absolutely no trading for their own account.

It is by no means clear that "globalization" poses a threat to such a market. The only significantly globalized market in operation in 1991 was the market for U.S. Treasury bonds and futures, traded in a major way in New York, Chicago, Tokyo, and London. The trading day began in Tokyo at 9:00 P.M. New York time and ran until 5:00 A.M. New York time; the trading day in London ran from 3:00 A.M. New York time to noon New York time; and in Chicago the trading day opened at 8:30 A.M. New

York time. The Japanese traded both bonds and futures from upstairs through screens; London and Chicago traded futures on exchanges and cash bonds through screens; New York traded cash bonds both through screens and on the New York Stock Exchange floor, which was not, however, a major market.

At places like Fundamental Brokers, Inc., the largest of the interdealer brokers, New York staff was in place by the opening of the London market to instruct the London staff. The operative word is "instruct." Even though FBI had senior brokers at work in London, it was understood that nobody not in the United States could really get a grip on the meaning of whatever developments were making the bond market move. U.S. Treasury obligations are a unique section of the securities market, because the Treasury is so dependent on foreign orders at its auctions and so much paper (probably more than a quarter of a trillion dollars' worth) is held by foreigners. Moreover, Treasury prices are highly dependent on foreign exchange fluctuations (as foreign exchange prices are dependent on interest rates), and foreign exchange is obviously a market where trading in foreign centers will be as well informed as trading in the United States.

For equities, the obvious truth is that spreads between bid and asked will always be wider in foreign markets than they are in the company's home country (just as they are wider here in the over-the-counter market for NYSE stocks that Jefferies & Co. operates in Los Angeles after the close of trading in New York). Information likely to influence the price of a company's stock will be more efficiently and accurately processed at home than abroad, and during trading hours rather than after them. No doubt there will be some trading in foreign stocks by people who like to do business in their own time zone, and in stocks of companies highly dependent on exports (the example used to be Britain's Jaguar before Ford bought it) where the market in the country that imports the product may be as significant as the home-country market. These will be exceptions, however. The danger to domestic securities markets is from index derivatives trading, which, like U.S. government bond trading, can go on worldwide twenty-four hours a day, and can be much cheaper for institutional players. Unless something is done to put friction between the futures and cash markets, such trading can push around the prices of all the securities in the index on any market where they are traded.

No one knows now whether screen-based trading can be a satisfactory substitute for trading floors. Except for CATS, which to date has been able to put computerized bids and offers into an auction on the floor as well as into the offices, today's screen markets are dealer markets. Abandonment of the floor led the British to a much less transparent market, because dealers upstairs, lacking the "feel" that people around a trading post get for the interest of others in their stocks, refused to publish to the world the fact that they were stuck with large positions. In the hope of holding business that was leaking off to nonmember market-makers, the London Stock Exchange had to permit the announcement of large trades to be delayed until the next day to give dealers a chance to lay off their excess inventory.

The Fault, Dear Brutus . . .

Are the exchange floors worth saving? The conventional, rather pious answer is that if it costs more to trade on an exchange floor than to trade upstairs through screens, the market will move upstairs and nothing can or should be done about it.

Steve Wunsch, whose Single Price Auction has been vigorously opposed by all the exchanges, goes much further, arguing that today's continuous auction markets through intermediaries deserve to be shot down:

> [I]ntermediary-dominated exchanges design markets that are fragmented, inefficient, unfair and unsafe, all of which increases dependence on intermediaries—and increases the regulatory challenge of protecting investors from abuse. Taken together, the memberships of the registered markets constitute a single intermediary cartel, whose natural role is maximizing intermediary revenues. In pursuit thereof: inefficiencies that widen spreads, impact, and volatility are both passively tolerated and actively built into the market structure; tilted playing fields that favor members over customers are preserved through rules, procedures, and active lobbying from Washington to Sacramento; and trading is fragmented into a dazzling array of times, places, and look-alike

instruments that separate investors like kids in a funhouse on the class trip. You know your friends are all there, but with the smoke, mirrors, mazes, moving floors and pop-out monsters (which, in continuous markets, are not always make-believe), finding them is another matter.

Gone are the days [wrote Wunsch, warming to his task], when one exchange traded standard securities at a standard time. This is the age of specialization. Hundreds of dealers make markets on various downstairs floors or upstairs block desks, at any time of day and frequently into the night. Customers' orders are splintered from the original securities into a seemingly infinite variety of tailor-made hybrids, derivatives, synthetics, and exotics, creating inefficiencies for the swift (i.e., cartel members) to arbitrage.[12]

One can indeed make a case that a single-price screen-based auction for several thousand stocks, once or twice a day, would be the best system for institutional trading, leaving the continuous auction market to the flow of orders from individual customers it was designed to process. That market would be too easily manipulable, however, by those who had a stake in moving the price at the institutional auction. The abuses Wunsch so vigorously describes (and it should be remembered that he ran the Kidder Peabody trading operation on the New York Futures Exchange before becoming the proprietor of Wunsch Auction Systems) are inventions of the 1980s, not inherent in the operation of trading floors or upstairs, screen-based continuous dealing. They highlight not the weaknesses of old-fashioned institutions but the dangers of allowing technology to alter markets without government oversight and regulation.

There are values in a centralized, open-outcry public market that cannot easily be duplicated electronically. On the other hand, a computer-based system has capacities for record-keeping that mortal memories cannot match. (When computers were new, Chicago University law professor Harry Kalven worried that "through computers, mankind may lose its benign capacity to forget.") In any event, it is not true that technology or even profitability will determine which systems are used for securities trading in the twenty-first century. All financial markets rely on a legal order for their fundamental stability, and governments are the providers of the legal order. Central banks guarantee payments systems and have much to say about the supply of credit. Limited liability corporations are state-chartered institutions. And rules of fair dealing need some degree of potential government enforcement, as the meat market needs inspectors to examine the scales.

We can decide through political process, and decide wisely, the parameters of our securities markets. The fault for the eighties was not in our stars, and the United States is not so weak financially or intellectually that it need accept foreign definitions of honest, open, broad, deep—and efficient—securities markets. We don't need and shouldn't want the patronage of the sorts of people who do their business hiding behind brass plates in the Cayman and Channel Islands. The purpose of securities markets is not to make a buck today but to provide the price information investors and bankers and producers need to plan their own contributions to the economic output of the society. If we look at the markets in that focus, we can reclaim them for the benefit of the larger capitalist enterprise that needs them. If we continue to ignore the public purposes of these markets, we will increasingly misallocate our real resources and eventually destroy the markets themselves.

Notes

1. Why the Stock Market Matters

1. Roger Lowenstein and George Anders, "Firms That Default Find Their Troubles May Have Just Begun," *Wall Street Journal*, 17 Apr. 1991.
2. See Martin Mayer, "Banks Should Keep the Banking Business," *American Banker*, 21 July 1987, 1. I am not saying that Michael Milken of Drexel Burnham did not take an interest in the borrowers' business, because in fact he became highly expert in almost every company he led up the garden path to Parnassus or down the garden path to ruin. But the institutions that bought the paper from him could not have cared less whether the company made bomb casings or sausage casings.
3. Craig S. Smith, "Abreast of the Market," *Wall Street Journal*, 10 Jan. 1991.
4. Edward A. Wyatt, "Trading in the Dark," *Barron's*, 6 Nov. 1989.
5. Gordon Crovitz, "One Cheer for the SEC," *Barron's*, 15 Oct. 1990.
6. Saul S. Cohen, "The Death of Securities Regulation," *Wall Street Journal*, 17 Jan. 1991.
7. Norma Cohen, "Counting the Cost of City Deregulation," *Financial Times*, 28 Oct. 1991.
8. Floyd Norris, "At the SEC, Another Move for Secrecy," *New York Times*, 13 Oct. 1991, Sec. 3, p. 1.

2. Making the Machine Run

1. Archie F. Tighe, "Round Lot Trading on the New York Stock Exchange," in Philip H. Lohman and Franc M. Ricciardi, ed., *Wall Street Explains Its Operations* (New York: Institute of Finance, 1951), 22 et seq.
2. Martin Mayer, *Wall Street: Men and Money* (New York: Harper & Bros., 1959 ed.), 62–63.
3. Richard A. Brealey, *Security Prices in a Competitive Market* (Boston: MIT Press, 1979), 91.
4. The numbers on institutional holdings are from the New York Stock Exchange *Institutional Investor Fact Book* for 1990; the exchange got them from the Federal Reserve Board "flow of funds" analysis, and noted dourly that these Fed figures get revised continually as history changes the minds of the Fed statisticians.
5. Martin Mayer, *New Breed on Wall Street* (New York: Macmillan, 1969), 21.
6. Securities and Exchange Commission, *Institutional Investor Study Report*, 10 Mar. 1971, vol. 3, 1941.
7. Laszlo Birinyi, Jr., *The Equity Desk* (New York: Salomon Brothers, Mar. 1987), 95.
8. Hurd Barch, *Wall Street: Security Risk* (Washington, D.C.: Acropolis Books, Ltd., 1971).
9. *Trends: An Analysis of Emerging Trends in the Securities Industry*, Securities Industry Association, New York, vol. 16, 7, 13 Nov. 1990, 5.
10. U.S. Congress, *Report of the Special Study of the Securities Markets of the Securities and Exchange Commission*, 88th Cong., 1st Sess., 1965, 385.
11. William Power, "Broker War Is On as Firms Grab Star Players with Big Bonuses," *Wall Street Journal*, 24 Oct. 1990.
12. Michael Siconolfi, "Prudential Official Concedes VMS Risks," *Wall Street Journal*, 18 June 1991.
13. Michael Lewis, *Liar's Poker* (New York: W. W. Norton, 1989), 167.
14. "Dean Witter Is Pushing Its In-House Mutual Funds," *Wall Street Journal*, 31 Jan. 1991.
15. Chris Welles, *The Last Days of the Club* (New York: E. P. Dutton, 1975).
16. James Sterngold, *Burning Down the House: How Greed, Deceit and Bitter Revenge Destroyed E. F. Hutton* (New York: Summit Books, 1990), 66–67.
17. William Dullforce, "Rudloff Castigates World's Bankers," *Financial Times*, 5 Feb. 1988.

3. The Adversarial Agent

1. Securities and Exchange Commission, *Statement on the Future Structure of the Securities Markets* (Washington, D.C.: GPO, 1972), 20.
2. *Hearings on H.R. 7852 and H.R. 8720 before the House Committee on Interstate and Foreign Commerce,* 73rd Cong., 2nd Sess., 1934, 124.
3. Cong. Rec., 73rd Cong., 1934, 2270–2271.
4. Securities and Exchange Commission, *Report on the Desirability and Advisability of the Complete Segregation of the Functions of Broker and Dealer* (Washington, D.C.: GPO, 1936), 109–110.
5. Securities and Exchange Commission Division of Trading and Exchanges, *Report on Floor Trading to the Commission* (Washington, D.C.: GPO, 15 Jan. 1945), 42.
6. Securities and Exchange Commission, *Report of the Special Study of Securities Markets,* H.R. Doc. No. 95, 88th Cong., 1st Sess., 1963, 210, 211.
7. Securities and Exchange Commission, *Adoption of Rule 19b-2 under the Securities Exchange Act of 1934: Governing the Utilization of Exchange Membership for Public Purposes,* 16 Jan. 1973, 122–123.
8. Sec. 11, Securities Exchange Act, 15 USC 78k.
9. Henny Sender, "The Client Comes Second," *Institutional Investor,* March 1987, 84; quotation from 86.
10. Anise C. Wallace, "Pension Managers Vow to Cut Trading Costs," *New York Times,* 20 Nov. 1987.
11. Statement of Donald M. Feuerstein concerning S. 470 and S. 488, at Hearing before the Subcommittee on Securities, U.S. Congress, Senate Committee on Banking, Housing and Urban Affairs, 21 Feb. 1973.
12. Remarks by William J. Casey, chairman, *Regulation and the Structure of the Securities Markets,* Securities and Exchange Commission, 30 Nov. 1972, 9.
13. "Morgan Stanley Hedge Team Stirs Street's Imagination," *Trading Systems Technology,* 14 Mar. 1982, 5.
14. Stephen A. Berkowitz, Dennis E. Logue, and Eugene A. Noser, Jr., "The Total Cost of Transactions on the NYSE," *The Journal of Finance,* 43, 1 (Mar. 1988): 97, quotation from p. 111.
15. *How to Hide Transaction Costs* (Santa Monica, CA.: Plexus Group, July 1990), Commentary No. 28, 2.
16. Securities and Exchange Commission, *Institutional Investor Study Report,* pt. 1, xxii.

17. *Institutional Investor,* Feb. 1973, 44.
18. Feuerstein, 17.
19. Ibid., 20.
20. *Institutional Investor Study Report,* xxv.

4. Living with the Futures

1. Stephen Fay, *Beyond Greed* (New York: Viking Press, 1982), 158.
2. John W. Labuszewski and John E. Nyhoff, *Trading Financial Futures* (New York: John Wiley & Sons, 1988), 5.
3. One should note in passing, however, that the daily "range" of the Dow—the published figures for that day's high and that day's low— are not in fact the top and bottom of the minute-by-minute recalculations of the average. Instead, they are the compilation of the high and the low for each stock. There was no moment in time when the Dow was at each day's high or low.
4. Rachel Davies, "Index Betting Debts Must Be Paid," *Financial Times,* 19 Mar. 1991.
5. Lawrence Harris, George Sofianos, and James E. Shapiro, "Program Trading and Intraday Volatility," New York Stock Exchange, mimeo.
6. Henry Kaufman, *Interest Rates, the Market, and the New Financial World* (New York: Times Books, 1986), 170, 171.
7. Sanford J. Grossman, "Institutional Investing and New Trading Technologies," *Market Volatility and Investor Confidence,* Report to the Board of Directors of the New York Stock Exchange, Inc. (New York: New York Stock Exchange, 1990), C2–9.
8. Harris, Sofianos, and Shapiro, "Program Trading," 11.
9. James F. Gammill, Jr., and André F. Perold, "The Changing Character of Stock Market Liquidity," *Journal of Portfolio Management* (Spring 1989): 13, 15.
10. Craig Torres, "Wall Street Finds a Gusher in Foreign Index Warrants," *Wall Street Journal,* 6 Nov. 1990.

5. Sure Things

1. New York Stock Exchange, Information Memo Number 8038, *Front-Running of Blocks,* 11 Sept. 1980, 1.
2. U.S. Congress, House Committee on Energy and Commerce, *Financial Market Regulatory Reform (Part 2): Hearings before the Subcommittee on Telecommunications and Finance,* 100th Cong., 2nd sess., 1988 (Serial 100–209), 43, 47–48.

3. Specifically it read: "If a member or person associated with a member or member organization executes or causes to be executed, for an account in which such member, member organization or person has a direct or indirect pecuniary interest or for an account with respect to which such person or member exercises investment discretion, any transactions described below to take advantage of material, nonpublic information which reasonably can be expected to have an immediate, favorable impact in relation to such transactions, such member or persons may be in violation of just and equitable principles of trade (Exchange Rule 476)."

4. The paragraph reads: "In addition, a member or person associated with a member organization who implements a proprietary market strategy involving a stock program (including transactions in Exchange Stock Portfolios) or stock index option transaction(s) and a related stock index futures transaction by executing the stock index futures trade(s) prior to the execution of the stock program or the stock index option transaction(s) will not necessarily be deemed to be in violation of this policy. However, if the member or person executes or causes to be executed a transaction in one market to take advantage of such member's or person's imminent transaction in a related market, that member or person may be engaging in manipulative activity."

5. "A 'Dangerous' Capital-Gains Tax," *Wall Street Journal,* 3 Oct. 1988.

6. Securities Exchange Act Release No. 7290 (9 Apr. 1964), 5.

7. *Technical Market Comment #1936,* Dean Witter Reynolds, Inc., 15 Dec. 1986.

8. "Program Trading's Latest Wrinkle," *Business Week,* 28 Aug. 1989, 72, quotation from 73.

9. Martin Mayer, "Some Watchdog," *Barron's,* 27 Dec. 1987, 14; Martin Mayer, *Markets* (New York: W. W. Norton, 1988), 86–87, 245.

10. Division of Economic Analysis and Division of Trading and Markets, *Interim Report on Stock Index Futures and Cash Market Activity During October 1987* (Washington, D.C.: Commodity Futures Trading Commission, 9 Nov. 1987), 61.

11. *The October 1987 Market Break,* A Report by the Division of Market Regulation, Securities and Exchange Commission, Feb. 1988, chap. 2, 38–39; chap. 3, 25–27; Appendix B, 33–40.

12. Kook & Co. v. Scheinman, Hochstin & Trotta, Inc., 414 F2d 93 (1969), @ 98.

13. Colema Realty Co. v. Bibow, 555 F. Supp 1030 (1983).

14. *The October 1987 Market Break,* chap. 3, 26, FN.

15. *Report of the Presidential Task Force on Market Mechanisms* (Washington, D.C.: GPO, Jan. 1988), 36, 65.

16. *Memorandum* to Chairman Ruder from Richard G. Ketchum re: Review of Market Volatility on January 8, 1988, 3.

17. New York Stock Exchange, Information Memo Number 88–13, 18 May 1988.

18. *Review of Stock Index Futures and Related Market Activity on April 14, 1988,* Commodity Futures Trading Commission, 1 June 1988, 12; Memorandum, *Implementation . . . of the New York Stock Exchange Restrictions on the Use of Automated Routing Systems for Index Arbitrage Programs,* Securities and Exchange Commission, 6 July 1988, Tables 2.5, 2.6. Broker/dealer "vast majority" is the author's extrapolation from the reports.

19. *Implementation of the New York Stock Exchange,* 16, FN 42.

20. Craig Torres, "Program Traders Move Off Exchanges," *Wall Street Journal,* 30 Aug. 1990.

21. Securities and Exchange Commission, *Report on the Feasibility and Desirability of the Complete Segregation of the Functions of Broker and Dealer* (Washington, D.C.: GPO, 1936), 100.

6. Fixed by Technology

1. *U.S. Government Securities: More Transaction Information and Investor Protection Measures Are Needed,* GAO report to Congressional committees, September 1990, GAO-GGD 90–114, Washington, D.C., 17.

2. Tom Herman, "The Next Voice These Traders Hear May Be a Computer," *Wall Street Journal,* 29 May 1991.

3. *U.S. Government Securities: More Transaction Information and Investor Protection Measures Are Needed,* 79, 80.

4. Martin Mayer, *Wall Street: Men and Money* (New York: Harper & Bros., 1959 ed.), 146.

5. U.S. Congress, Office of Technology Assessment, *Electronic Bulls and Bears: U.S. Securities Markets and Information Technology* (Washington, D.C.: GPO, 1990), 136.

6. William Davidson, "Paris Traders Call for Reform," *Financial Times,* 8 July 1991.

7. Karl Marx, *Capital,* ed. Friedrich Engels, vol. 3, translated from the first German edition by Ernest Untermann (Chicago: Charles H. Kerr, 1909), 575 FN.

8. Ernest N. Paolino, *William Henry Seward and American Foreign*

Policy (Ithaca, NY: Cornell University Press, 1973), 76 et seq.

9. "The Internationalisation of Trading," a talk by James L. Cochrane to the *Financial Times* Conference Organization meeting on the European Securities Markets in the '90s, London, 22 Apr. 1991, 6 et seq.

7. The Vanishing Government

1. Nicholas Wolfson, "Investment Banking," in Roy Schotland, ed., *Abuse on Wall Street,* A Twentieth Century Fund Report (Westport, CT: Quorum Books, 1980), 404–405.

2. James Sterngold, *Burning Down the House: How Greed, Deceit and Bitter Revenge Destroyed E. F. Hutton* (New York: Summit Books, 1990), 70.

3. *E. F. Hutton Investment Series, Inc.,* Investment Company Act Release No. 12079, 4 Dec. 1961. Noblesse oblige: Once Hutton had been given this privilege to deceive, other brokers gained similar exemptions.

4. David A. Vise and Steve Coll, *Eagle on the Street* (New York: Scribners, 1991).

5. Martin Mayer, *Today and Tomorrow in America* (New York: Harper & Row, 1975).

6. *Report of the President's Task Force on Market Mechanisms,* otherwise "the Brady Report," Washington, D.C., Jan. 1988, 65.

7. S. Rep. No. 75 to accompany S. 249, 94th Cong., 1st Sess., 1975, 100. Emphasis added.

8. Securities Exchange Act of 1934, as amended to 19 Nov. 1988, Section 11(a)-3-b.

9. "Report to the Securities and Exchange Commission by the Advisory Committee on a Central Market System," Washington, D.C., 6 Mar. 1973, mimeo, 9.

10. *Short-Selling Activity in the Stock Market: The Effects on Small Companies and the Need for Regulation,* Hearings before the House Committee on Government Operations, 101st Congress, 1st Sess., 6 Dec. 1989 (Washington, D.C.: GPO, 1991), 385.

11. *New York Times,* 3 June 1991, Sec. 3.

12. Letter from Robert E. Rubin of Goldman Sachs and Richard B. Fisher of Morgan Stanley to Elizabeth Hanford Dole, 26 Feb. 1990; *ERISA Issues Arising from Soft Dollar Arrangements,* Paper submitted to the Department of Labor by Goldman, Sachs & Co. and Morgan Stanley Group, Inc., 1990, executive summary, 2; introduction, 2; conclusions, 34.

13. *ERISA Issues Arising from Soft Dollar Arrangements,* 15.
14. "Where's the Beef?" special commentary, Rochdale Securities Corporation, New York, July 1990, 5.
15. *The USSR/NYSE Seminar: Stock Exchanges and Their Role in Financial Markets* (New York: NYSE, 1991), 124–125.
16. S. L. Mintz, "The SEC Shakes the Money Tree," *Corporate Finance,* Mar. 1989, 32.
17. Deborah Hargreaves, "Portal Proves an Ignored Honeypot," *Financial Times,* 3 Oct. 1990.
18. Stephen Labaton, "U.S. May Ease Rules Affecting Foreign Stocks," *New York Times,* 5 June 1991, p. 1, quotation from p. 21.
19. Dissenting Statement of Commissioner Fleischman, SEC Docket 7 June 1991, mimeo, 61, 63.
20. Meinard v. Salmon, 249 NY (1928), 458, @ 464.
21. Section 11(b), Analysis of Additional Conversion Opportunities for Percentage Orders. Brief submitted to the SEC by Richard P. Bernard, 6 May 1985, 12.

8. Remote and Opaque

1. *NYSE Fact Book 1991* (New York: NYSE, 1991), 79, 77.
2. Laszlo Birinyi, Jr., *The Equity Desk* (New York: Salomon Brothers, March 1987), 85.
3. John G. Cragg and Burton G. Malkiel, *Expectations and Share Prices* (Chicago, University of Chicago Press, 1982).
4. Securities and Exchange Commission, *Institutional Investor Study Report,* 10 Mar. 1971, 2530.
5. Louis Lowenstein, *What's Wrong with Wall Street* (Reading, MA.: Addison-Wesley, 1988), 82–85.
6. "A Dangerous Capital Gains Tax," *Wall Street Journal,* 3 Oct. 1988.
7. *Institutional Investor Study Report,* transmittal letter signed by Commissioner Robert Smith, Washington, D.C., 10 Mar. 1971, xxiii.
8. "Capitalism and the Saver," *Financial Times,* 12 June 1991.
9. L. J. Davis, "When AT&T Plays Hardball," *New York Times Business World,* 9 June 1991, 14, quotation from p. 31.
10. "The Death of Securities Regulation," *Wall Street Journal,* 17 Jan. 1991.
11. Dissenting Statement of Commissioner Fleischman, SEC Docket 7 June 1991, mimeo, 62.
12. R. Steven Wunsch, *Auction Countdown* (New York: Wunsch Auction Systems, Inc., 10 June 1991), 2.

Index